HIDDEN JOY

in a DARK CORNER

HIDDEN JOY

in a DARK CORNER

The Transforming Power of God's Story

Wendy Jer. 33:3

Wendy Blight

MOODY PUBLISHERS
CHICAGO

Editor: Karyn Hecht
Interior Design: Ragont Design
Cover Design: Brand Navigation
Cover Image: Getty Images: 200449146-001
Author Photo: Ralph Melvin & Associates

Library of Congress Cataloging-in-Publication Data
Blight, Wendy.
  Hidden joy in a dark corner : the transforming power of God's story / Wendy Blight.
    p. cm.
  Includes bibliographical references.
  ISBN 978-0-8024-1496-0
  1. Blight, Wendy. 2. Christian biography—United States. 3. Rape—Religious aspects—Christianity. I. Title.
  BR1725.B578A3 2009
  277.3'083092--dc22
  [B]

                                                    2008039778

We hope you enjoy this book from Moody Publishers. Our goal is to provide high-quality, thought-provoking books and products that connect truth to your real needs and challenges. For more information on other books and products written and produced from a biblical perspective, go to www.moodypublishers.com or write to:

Moody Publishers
820 N. LaSalle Boulevard
Chicago, IL 60610

3 5 7 9 10 8 6 4

Printed in the United States of America

To my husband, Monty: thank you
for your unconditional love
and unwavering commitment
every step of this journey

CONTENTS

With
GRATITUDE . . .

TO MY TWO CHILDREN, Lauren and Bo: You fill my life with incredible joy and laughter. Your love, prayers, and sacrifice through the writing of this manuscript have been precious gifts that I will forever treasure.

To my parents, John and Connie Rotty, who instilled in me the belief that I could do anything I set my mind to. And to my in-laws, Ed and Carolyn Blight, for faithfully covering our family in prayer before they ever knew me.

To Moody Publishers for believing in this project. Because of your commitment to feed the Word of God to hungry souls, many broken and hurting hearts will be healed and restored.

To my editors, Jennifer Lyell, Karyn Hecht, and Pam Pugh. Jennifer, for deeming this project worthy of publication, your dedication to protect the heart of my story, and your continued encouragement each step of the way. Karyn, for the hours you faithfully invested your gifts and talents into this manuscript. Pam, for your words of encouragement, your invaluable advice, and the laughter we shared along the way. You make me smile!

To President Herbert H. Reynolds and Reverend Mark Craig for introducing me to God's Word and showing me that it is full of promises meant for me today.

To Jan Harrison for passionately living out your faith before my eyes. Your passion for God's Word inspired me and gave me a hunger and thirst for Truth that has forever changed my life.

To my heart sisters, Karen Cauthen, Lisa Allen, and Lendy Jones: God used you more than you will ever know to encourage and inspire me on my journey of healing.

To Lisa Sheltra for walking through every page of this book with me. You gave me valuable critique and encouragement and helped me find the right words to convey the message that filled my heart.

To Bobbie, Robert, and Erik Wolgemuth for your willingness to take a chance on a new author. Bobbie, I am forever grateful for your belief in my story and your encouragement every step of the way.

To the South Charlotte Women's Bible study for allowing me the privilege of studying God's Word with you these past five years. We have prayed together, laughed together, cried together, and, most of all, grown together. You are the best, and I love you all!

To the Young Women's Bible Study and Lynn Pitts for giving me my first platform from which to teach. It has been my greatest joy and privilege to walk alongside you as we opened the Word of God together and experienced the incredible hope and power it holds.

Finally, to my many friends and family who took precious time to read all or part of this manuscript and provide valuable insight and suggestions.

Our Journey
BEGINS

I will give you a new heart and put a new spirit in you; I will remove from you your heart of stone and give you a heart of flesh.

—EZEKIEL 36:26

HAVE YOU EVER BEEN the victim of someone's violent behavior? Have you felt like someone ripped away all you had in this world? Have you felt like your life is spinning out of control and you do not know how you can survive another day? Have you experienced a physical or emotional pain so deep that nothing can soothe the hurt?

I have. These questions describe how I lived for years after my terrifying experience.

Circumstances can destroy everything you know to be good and true. It happened to me over twenty years ago when an armed, masked man hiding inside my home raped me. It has been a difficult story to write, one that takes me back to a desperate time. Every line I write reminds me of the years of terror, despair, and hopelessness in which I lived. I wondered whether I really wanted to travel back in time to that place, to that pain. Yet I feel compelled to tell you my story, the full story, so I can share the beautiful hope and new life given to me . . . and available for you. There was a time when being a rape victim defined my life and left me physically void, cocooned in a prison of fear. It stole my every hope and dream. But God's love and His Word set my heart free. I learned that within the confines of God's story, nothing had been stolen from me, but rather everything was given to me. My life, which felt so out of control, was in reality in complete control—God's control.

In this book, I will share the lessons I learned from the pages of God's incredible story: the Bible. My prayer is that you too will see that His story is not merely a book but a love letter written especially for you. It transformed my life and infused me with a new power, one I had never experienced before. As you journey through this book, open your heart to what God has to speak to you. Consider *your* story and allow the powerful Truths that unfold—His Truths —to affect your life and forever change you, just as it has forever changed me.

My journey is far from over. In fact, you are now a part of it as I share my story with you. As you turn the pages of this book, please know that I have prayed for you. Each time I sat down to write, I asked the Lord to give me words, stories, and verses that would touch the hearts of the women who would read them.

God led you to choose this book because He has a personal message for you . . . powerful Truths He wants to teach you . . . amazing love He wants to reveal to you . . . everlasting hope He wants to offer you. Listen for His voice. Search for the blessings hidden in your brokenness. Are you ready? Turn the page and let's begin our journey together.

CHAPTER ONE

Valley of WEEPING

*When they walk through the Valley of Weeping it
will become a place of springs where pools of blessing
and refreshment collect after rains!*

—PSALM 84:6 (TLB)

IT WAS SUPPOSED TO BE the happiest time of my life . . .
the summer after my senior year in college . . . a time for new beginnings. I was engaged to be married and preparing to start my
first "real job." Things were working out exactly as I had planned.

In early June, just days before I was to begin my new job, I
spent a leisurely afternoon with friends by the pool. It was a typical Texas summer day, 95 degrees and muggy. We were celebrating
the end of one journey and the beginning of another. As the afternoon wore on, we made evening plans, and the pool emptied.

My roommates had left earlier that day to go out of town for
the weekend, so I went back to my apartment alone. Our apartment had two entrances, one a sliding glass door in the back, facing the pool, and the other a front door, facing the parking lot.

As I entered my back door and walked toward the stairs near
the front of the apartment, I noticed that someone had locked the

front door, which was unusual because we never locked the door except at night. *I don't remember locking this.* A tingling sensation ran through me. You know that feeling you get when something does not feel right? Forgetting it rather quickly, I slowly climbed the stairs to the second floor, daydreaming, my mind flooded with memories of the last four years.

When I reached the top of the stairs, a man wearing a bandana over his face with holes cut out for his eyes and mouth confronted me. The stranger was dressed in long pants, tennis shoes, and a T-shirt. He wore leather hunting gloves and wielded a large knife with a thick blade. *This isn't real. Surely this is a joke. Who would do such a thing?* It was the ice-cold stare behind his piercing blue eyes that jolted me into reality. He told me not to make a sound or he would cut me. He grabbed me by the arm and told me he would kill me if I did not do everything he said. This was no joke.

In those moments, everything within me died.

Every move calculated, he walked me back down the stairs. At first, I felt relief because I thought he was hiding from the police or wanted money. Within seconds, I knew he had other plans. The masked man dragged me around the apartment, locking every door and window and closing every blind. As we stood in front of the sliding glass door overlooking the pool, I pled in my mind for the few friends left at the pool to glance my way and see this masked stranger holding a knife to my throat. The closing of that last blind snuffed out any hope I had of rescue. He ordered me to take the phone off the hook and pushed me back toward the stairs. As we passed the front door, I reached for the lock. Before I could turn it, he grabbed me and threw me against the wall. He pressed the knife against my throat. The cold blade touched my skin. My captor then pushed me up the stairs, still holding the knife at my neck.

As we reached the top of the stairs, I turned and begged the man to leave, promising not to tell anyone. I told him that I had no idea who he was and would have no way of identifying him. He shoved me into my bedroom, ordering me to shut up and not say another word. I knew now there was no escape; I was his captive. He stared at me and told me to undress with my back toward him. He forced me onto the bed. He placed a washcloth over my face and kept it there the entire time. I remember feelings of complete humiliation, shame, and vulnerability as if it were yesterday.

I begged him to leave. Terror filled my body, unlike anything I have ever experienced. My captor dug the knife into my neck. His face inches from mine, he whispered, "Say another word, and I will kill you."

In those moments, everything within me died. I was an empty tomb. I experienced pain so deep that it seared my soul. He touched me all over. He forced himself into me over and over again. Involuntary cries came from my mouth, and with each cry, my attacker grew angrier. Finally, he climbed off me. *Could this nightmare really be over?* He stood up, zipped his pants, leaned in close to my face, and whispered with an intense evil, "I know where you live. If you tell anyone, I will return, and I will kill you." He told me not to move until I had counted to 100. He continued to threaten me as he walked out of the room and down the stairs.

I lay on my bed, counting to 100, naked, weeping, not knowing if the masked man had actually left the apartment. I was terrified that he was tricking me by waiting downstairs. Finally, I mustered the courage to get off the bed. I wrapped my towel around me and walked down the stairs. With each step, I grew more and more anxious. When I reached the last step, I felt a surge of relief, flung open the now-unlocked front door, and ran out.

For a moment, I stood alone outside, sobbing. *Where would I go? Who should I tell? Would he come back? Why me? What did I do?* Finally, barefoot, shaking, and holding the towel tightly around me, I ran, ran as if my life depended on it, to my fiancé's apartment. He lived a few doors down and around the corner. I burst through the door. Words poured from my mouth, but I made no sense. Hearing the words *mask* and *knife*, Monty and his roommates raced out the door toward my apartment. However, I knew the masked man was gone. I had waited too long. When they came back, Monty wrapped his arms around me, but I felt nothing. I did not want anyone to touch me or hold me ever again. They told me that I needed to call the police. However, the rapist's words, his threats to return and kill me if I told anyone, reverberated in my mind.

After I called the police, Monty took me to the local hospital emergency room. When we arrived, we walked up to the triage desk. The receptionist asked, "May I help you?"

"Yes," I replied, "I need to see a doctor."

"What are you here for?" she asked matter-of-factly.

As those words rolled off her tongue, I hesitated and then spoke three words I never thought I would utter: "I was raped." As the words came out, shame and humiliation surged through my body.

We waited for what seemed an eternity. A nurse finally came and escorted me to a cold, sterile examination room. She introduced herself and asked me to wait a few more moments while she went to retrieve the rape kit. As I waited, I recounted the minutes before I climbed the stairs of my apartment. *Why didn't I stop when I saw the locked door? Why didn't I try harder to escape when he took me back downstairs? Why didn't I fight back?* The questions flooded my mind, one after another. I felt as if I could not breathe.

The nurse returned, bringing me back to reality. She placed a large piece of crinkly white paper on the floor and instructed me to stand on it and remove all my clothing. The paper would capture any evidence the perpetrator may have left behind, she explained. Then, handing me a white gown, she instructed me to put it on and to lie down on an exam table covered with the same crinkly paper. It was cold against my skin.

Next, the nurse asked me to raise my knees and place my feet in the stirrups. She proceeded with a painful and complicated exam, further humiliating me by pulling vaginal hairs and taking samples. Next, she initiated a barrage of questions, asking me to explain detail by detail what had occurred over the previous terror-filled hours. As I recounted the events, it seemed like a dream, as if I were living outside my body. *Is this real? Am I really here in this room? Where is he? What is he doing? Is he thinking about me?*

When the exam was complete, there was a knock at the door. My heart pounded as I watched a male doctor walk into the room. He began another lengthy interrogation. Quietly I answered his questions, explaining for the third time the opening scene of this nightmare. The young doctor outlined the steps I needed to take from this point and what to look for in case the man had STDs or in the event I might become pregnant. *Pregnant!* I had not even gone there in my mind. I felt myself slipping away. It was all happening so fast, and I could not cope. I wanted to leap off the table and run, run and never look back.

After the doctor completed his exam, the police officer assigned to my case came into the room and informed me that I had to return to my apartment to meet with the CSIs. When we arrived, I encountered another round of probing questions, once again reliving my nightmare. One of the officers asked me to fill out an incident report. This required that I write down the entire incident. "Every detail," he said. "Leave nothing out." I could not even hold the pen, so my dear friend Karen wrote while I recounted every horrid moment. I watched them take my things, one by one: my bathing suit, comforter, sheets, towel, and washcloth. Black fingerprint dust covered everything in the apartment. After the crime team left, I collapsed, weeping, wondering when I would wake up from this nightmare. Though surrounded by friends who cared for me and wanted to help, I felt utterly alone.

Fear became my driving force.

Total exhaustion set in. I do not remember the rest of the day.

I do know that I never wanted to return to my apartment . . . ever! All I wanted was to start my day over again . . . but this time when I saw the locked door, I would run and never climb those stairs.

In the days that followed, no one around me knew what to say or how to act . . . even my closest friends. Everyone had the best of intentions, but no words comforted me. I remember walking across campus and people quickly looking away when they caught my gaze. It was so painful that I felt even more isolated.

That single hour forever changed my life. My dreams were shattered. The joyful anticipation of my wedding and life as a newlywed vanished. Where there once had been happiness, there was hopelessness. Endless tears filled my days. The nights were worse, sleepless and filled with terror. Nightmares and frightening reruns of my rape permeated the few hours of sleep I did get. Every time I closed my eyes, I saw his masked face, his blue eyes, and the knife. In my dreams, blood covered the knife. Often I watched television all night to avoid closing my eyes. The rising sun, which had always brought the hope and excitement of a new day, now illuminated my tearstained face. I had the overwhelming feeling that I could not endure another day. I was emotionally drained and physically exhausted. I reached the desperate place of wanting to end my life. It was simply too difficult to live each day in the fear that imprisoned me.

My life before the rape felt as if all my dreams were coming true. I could have been the popular girl in the typical made-for-TV movie who had it all. I had pledged Kappa Kappa Gamma, which had blessed me with an incredible circle of friends. I dated a handsome fraternity boy who played football for Baylor. My peers voted me a Baylor Beauty and a Homecoming Princess my senior year. I graduated with honors. To top it all off, I was engaged to my handsome football player, and I was days away from starting my first job. Baylor University's Development office had selected me along with two other graduates for a twelve-month paid internship to serve as ambassadors for the university and travel the country representing the school. Life truly was perfect.

My life after the rape felt completely different. Fear became my driving force. I was afraid to be alone, even within the confines of my own home: afraid to enter empty rooms, afraid to climb to the top of any staircase, afraid to be anywhere alone with a man other than Monty, and afraid to sleep because of the nightmares. Fear consumed my every waking moment. For months after my rape, I refused to take a shower unless someone sat in the bathroom with me from beginning to end.

I also developed an irrational fear of men, especially those who fit the profile of my rapist. I spent days, months, even years after my rape looking for men who fit his description. *Could he be the one?* I remember one cocktail party in particular. I was mingling with friends. Across the room, I saw a young man about the same height, weight, and eye color of the man who raped me. I immediately froze, unable to function. *Could it be him?* I knew this particular man had been at Baylor when I was there. I made my girlfriend take me home immediately. I could not be in the same room with him . . . just in case he was the one. These kinds of irrational thoughts controlled my life.

Would I ever recover from this violation? It felt as if I would live in this prison for the rest of my life. Both the doctor and the police officers strongly suggested I meet with a rape counselor. I avoided doing so for as long as I could, but I finally succumbed. I first visited a psychologist who seemed only to talk in circles and to ask many questions without providing answers. Not long after, I attended a group session at the local rape crisis center with other rape victims. Most of the women in this group were in various stages of depression. They only added to my sense of hopelessness. *Was this what my life would be? Would I be like them?* After one visit, I never returned.

I longed to hear something—anything—from God. I was so angry with Him. Night after night I lay in bed, tears soaking my pillow. *Why didn't You protect me? Why didn't You warn me? Why did*

You abandon me? Why would You let this happen to me? Friends, especially Christians, would say to me, "God has a purpose. God will bring good out of this." I knew they meant well, but how could they utter such ridiculous statements? No good would ever come from this! What possible purpose could there be for the unspeakable acts that a vile man committed against me?

I was in a deep valley unlike any other I had ever experienced. I felt so alone. No one, not a single soul, understood the depths of my pain and my despair. No one knew the terror I lived with each day. No one knew . . . my loneliness, my helplessness, my hopelessness.

CHAPTER TWO

Why Did God ALLOW THIS?

*Call to me and I will answer you and tell you great
and unsearchable things you do not know.*

—JEREMIAH 33:3

MY HEART GREW COLD. I put a wall around myself, not letting anyone or anything penetrate it. I calculated my every move to ensure nothing like that ever happened to me again. I immediately moved in with Monty and his roommates. Among the four of them, they made sure I was never alone. I had convinced myself that as long as I was never alone, I would be safe. No one would hurt me again. I began my new job and tried to resume a normal life. Unanswered questions filled my mind in the days and weeks following my attack. *Who is he? Why did he choose me? Did I do something to attract him? Where is he now? Why could they not find him? Is he watching me?* The police occasionally updated me on the progress of their investigation, but the news was never good. They located the mask, knife, and gloves, but the rapist left no fingerprints. There were no leads.

As summer passed, it became painfully obvious the authorities were never going to find the man who did this. To make matters worse, Monty would be graduating in August and moving to Dallas to start his new job. I could not imagine how I was going to survive in Waco without him. He was my protector. I relied on him for everything. My rapist was still out there, and I obsessively believed he would keep his word and return to hurt me.

In September, Monty left for his new job, and I reluctantly stayed behind to complete my internship. I moved into a new apartment with three new roommates; they were my friends as well as sorority sisters. I spent the first few evenings after he moved huddled in the corners of my apartment, terrified at what my future might hold. It sounds irrational now, but my feelings and my fears were real to me. My roommates did their best to support me. They tried to ensure I was never alone, but they had their own lives. If they promised to be home at a certain time but were late, I would sit alone, terrified, anxiously waiting for their return.

I felt betrayed by God and could not understand what I could have done to deserve such a horrible punishment. I had thought that as long as I believed in God, lived a good life, and did the best that I could, God would protect me from the bad things.

I vividly remember one desperate night sitting on my bathroom floor, cradling my Bible in my arms, and crying out to God: *If this Book is true, if You love me, if You want the best for me, if You have a plan and purpose for my life, then You have got to show me. Because right now, I can't trust You, and I don't believe You!*

Where had God been that late summer afternoon in Waco, Texas? There seemed to be only three viable answers. One, God did not have the power to stop the rape. He wanted to protect me but could not. If that were true, what good is He? Two, God is all-powerful, but He did not care enough to intervene. He set this world in motion and then walked away to leave us to our own devices. If that were true, why should I look to Him for answers? Finally, God is all-powerful, and He loves me greatly, yet He allowed this to happen anyway. This answer scared me the most. God knew what was happening, could have stopped it, but did not. Why?

I became obsessed with finding the answers to my questions, but I had no idea where to begin. I took a long, hard look at my circumstances and realized that I was processing everything through the lens of my pain, my hurt, and my fear. I decided I needed to find a different lens, God's lens, through which to see my circumstances. To do that, I needed someone who knew God better than I did.

> *Although I knew Bible stories, I saw them as just that—stories. They had no practical application in my life.*

I went to my dear friend Lendy. Her faith had always been an example to me throughout college. I knew she had a strong relationship with God and would know how to find His perspective. Despite her close walk with God, she did not have the answers to my questions. However, she did give me insight into looking at life's circumstances through God's lens versus my lens. She explained how human beings base their perspective on what happens in the here and now. But God sees things differently. God transcends time. Clocks and calendars are irrelevant to Him. She told me that God saw my life all at once. He knew the day I was born and the day I would die, and He knew every moment in between. Every day was planned and every moment ordained to accomplish His purpose and calling on my life. She read to me from Psalm 139:16—"You saw me before I was born and scheduled each day of my life before I began to breathe. Every day was recorded in your Book!" (TLB). Although I did not fully comprehend everything she was saying, she said enough to convince me that I needed to continue my search for God's perspective on my circumstances.

She put a Bible and a daily devotional titled *Be Still and Know* by Millie Stamm in my hand and promised that if I faithfully pursued God for answers, He would provide. Before we ended our time together, she prayed with me, and then she said the strangest thing. She told me not to be intimidated as I embarked on my quest for answers because God wanted me to understand my circumstances and see them from His perspective. She told me that God desired a personal relationship with me and all that I needed to do was get to know Him the same way I would get to know a new friend.

Sounds strange, does it not? The same God who created the heavens and the earth desires a personal relationship with you and me. Yet, it is true. In John 15, Jesus refers to all those who believe in Him as His friends. So how do you get to know a friend? Although the following story jumps ahead many years, it illustrates this truth.

When we first moved to Charlotte, I met a wonderful group of women in my neighborhood who invited my children and me to join their playgroup. On my first visit, I met a beautiful young mom named Sharon. She had three children, and I had two. Our daughters were both five years old and shared the name Lauren. I had a one-year-old son, and she was pregnant with her third child. Our early conversations centered on the basics: Where did you grow up? How did you get to Charlotte? Where did you go to college? How did you meet your husband? What did you do before you had children?

After a few months, Sharon invited our family to her home for dinner. It was an incredible evening. Monty and I had left rich and wonderful friendships in Dallas and missed special times like that with friends. As the evening progressed, we learned more about our families, our backgrounds, and our personalities.

Over the months, as we spent time together and got to know each other better, our relationship deepened. Our conversations became more intimate and vulnerable. We shared our hopes, dreams, fears, and frustrations. We prayed for and encouraged each other. Even now, if I need a friend in the middle of the night, I call Sharon. If she needs a trusted heart to share a secret with, she picks up the phone. Our friendship is such that no matter what we share, we can be confident it stays just between us.

That is what Lendy meant when she said I needed to get to know God as a friend. If I wanted to learn more about God, I had to spend time with Him. She said the best way to know God is to meet Him in His Word every day. I decided to follow her advice. My grandmother had given me a Bible as a Christmas gift just months before. I began to read it. I knew the familiar stories of Noah's ark, Joseph and the coat of many colors, Moses and the Ten Commandments, and Jonah and the fish. I had learned them as a young child growing up in the church. I knew God as the Creator of the universe, the One who brought the flood and gifted the world with rainbows, the One who parted the Red Sea, and the One who authored the Ten Commandments.

Although I knew the stories, I saw them as just that—stories. They had no practical application in my life. Nevertheless, my skewed perspective of the Bible's relevance, or lack thereof, changed as God brought godly men and women into my life. Of course, at the time I did not see them as people brought by God to speak Truth into my life. I saw them as nice people trying to help me through a very difficult time.

My first "God appointment" was with the president of Baylor University, Herbert Reynolds. A few days after my attack, his secretary called and said that Dr. Reynolds would like to visit with me if I felt up to it. With trepidation, I accepted his invitation.

As his secretary opened the door to his office, I was awed by its majesty. Richly colored tapestry draped each window. Magnificent paintings lined the walls. Hundreds of books filled the shelves. Dr. Reynolds sat behind a beautifully hand-carved mahogany desk. He rose from his chair and extended me his arm. He gave me the warmest hug I ever remembered receiving. I felt almost safe in that moment. Dr. Reynolds motioned for me to sit in one of the stately antique chairs across from his desk. Although his office was imposing, he immediately put me at ease. His eyes were gentle and his words filled with compassion. He asked if there was anything I needed and offered any assistance he could give.

After talking for quite a while, he turned the conversation to my faith. In his questions, I sensed a genuine concern for my well-being. One by one, I answered. Yes, I am a Christian. Yes, I attend a local church. Yes, I have a personal relationship with Christ. *Wait . . . there is that* relationship *word again. What does he mean by that? Personal relationship?* Well, I was not exactly sure what he meant, but I was certain yes was the correct answer for a graduate of his Baptist university.

> *My baffled expression must have given away my confusion.*

Dr. Reynolds proceeded to share a personal experience with me. He had recently survived a massive heart attack. He spoke of his relationship with Christ carrying him through that difficult time. Near the end of our visit, he handed me a slip of paper. Written on it was his "life verse." He quoted it from memory: "For I am convinced that neither death nor life, neither angels nor demons, neither the present nor the future, nor any powers, neither height nor depth, nor anything else in all creation, will be able to separate us from the love of God that is in Christ Jesus our Lord" (Romans 8:38–39).

Life verse? I had no idea what he meant. My baffled expression must have given away my confusion. He explained that a life verse is a promise from the Bible given specifically to a person by God. Sometimes the verse points a person toward God's plan or direction for her life, or sometimes it provides a powerful truth or promise in the midst of a struggle or trial. I took the verse he gave me and promised to read it.

At the time, this verse meant nothing more than a sweet gesture. After all, it was Dr. Reynolds's life verse, not mine. However, later that night as I lay in bed, I opened my Bible, found the verse, and read it repeatedly, as if it would magically make everything better. My eyes wandered down to the end of the page. For the first time, I noticed there were footnotes in my Bible. These footnotes directed me to other verses in the Bible. Intrigued, I read the referenced verses. These verses introduced me to a new concept of God I had never heard of before . . . His sovereignty.

Sovereignty sounded so intimidating. When I looked up its definition, I found that it simply meant one who possesses supreme power. The verses referred to God as a King, but not just any king. The Bible calls Him the "King of all the earth" (Psalm 47:7). It said He is the "blessed controller of all things" (1 Timothy 6:15 PHILLIPS).

Another verse states that God has control over all circumstances: "The earth is the Lord's, and everything in it, the world, and all who live in it; for he founded it upon the seas and established it upon the waters" (Psalm 24:1–2). The verses exalt God above all things. One verse proclaims that "all authority in heaven and on earth has been given to [him]" (Matthew 28:18). Another says, "Through him all things were made; without him nothing was made that has been made" (John 1:3).

I was familiar with the story of creation in Genesis, but I had never thought of its profound significance in my own life. For the first time, I pondered all of God's creation and His hand in it. I marveled at how He created this vast universe: the planets, the sun, the moon, and the stars. Yet at the same time, He designed the tiniest, most delicate snowflake that falls to the earth. He gave the turtle a shell for protection; He made birds with hollow bones and feathers so they can fly; He made butterflies so they hatch from chrysalises, and He designed a precious baby to grow and develop in his or her mother's womb.

Even more amazing is that the Bible refers to God as the "author of life" (Acts 3:15). He created every living being. He knows each of His creations intimately: "Not one sparrow . . . can fall to the ground without your Father knowing it. And the very hairs of your head are all numbered. So don't worry! You are more valuable to him than many sparrows" (Matthew 10:29–30 TLB). I could not believe it. The very hairs on my head are numbered! Isaiah 40:26 says, "Lift your eyes and look to the heavens: Who created all these?

He who brings out the starry host one by one, and calls them each by name. Because of his great power and mighty strength, not one of them is missing." God Himself created every star in the universe and called each one by name.

According to Scripture, there is no doubt that God has authority over all things that happen on this earth, including what happens to you and me. This means that there are no accidents. There are no mistakes. Nothing happens to any one of us that does not first pass through God's sovereign hand.

This made absolutely no sense to me. If these verses were true, and God controlled my circumstances, then He allowed my rape. He could have intervened and stopped the evil, but He chose not to. Why? How could He watch this vulgar, repulsive, and cruel act while sitting on His throne in heaven and do absolutely nothing? This made me angrier with God than when I started my quest. How could God have allowed this man to perpetrate such a horrific crime against one of His children, one whom He claimed to love and whom He created?

Though confused and angry, something compelled me onward. The verses moved from God's sovereignty to His wisdom. The word *wisdom* derives from the Hebrew word *chokmah*. It generally refers to a person's technical skills or special abilities.[1] However, another meaning is "the knowledge and the ability to make right choices at the opportune time."[2]

Numerous verses declaring God's wisdom jumped off the pages of my Bible:

God made the earth by his power; he founded the world by his wisdom and stretched out the heavens by his understanding. (Jeremiah 10:12)

Oh, the depth of the riches of the wisdom and knowledge of God! How unsearchable his judgments, and his paths beyond tracing out! (Romans 11:33)

By wisdom the Lord laid the earth's foundations, by understanding he set the heavens in place; by his knowledge the deeps were divided, and the clouds let drop the dew.
(Proverbs 3:19–20)

Grasping the true meaning of these verses was beyond my human comprehension. God "spoke" the entire universe into being. Scripture clearly says that in the beginning the earth was "formless and empty," a shapeless mass (Genesis 1:2). God stepped into time and laid the foundations of the earth. He painted the horizons, gathered the waters to create dry land, placed the sun in the sky, and perfectly ordered the planets around it. He brought forth vegetation of every kind. He filled the earth with living creatures, each according to its own kind and each created with its own unique design and purpose. On the sixth day, God created His crown of creation, humankind (Genesis 1:1–27). On the seventh day, when He rested, there was perfect order.[3]

I marvel at how His created order continues to this day. Charlotte, North Carolina, is one of the greatest places to observe God's order at work. In March, the entire city explodes in vivid color. It begins as the first blossoms appear on the Bradford pear trees. They cover the streets of Charlotte like a blanket of freshly fallen snow. Next, delicate cherry blossoms make an appearance, as do colorful tulips, then the yellow daffodils, and finally blooming hydrangea bushes in varying shades of red, pink, and blue emerge on every street corner. Everywhere I turn, the glory of God's created order greets me. They bloom without fail, year after year after year.

Months later, fall arrives, and the beauty of the Carolina countryside is unmatched. Canopies of gold, red, and yellow leaves overlay every street. Within a few months, the grass dies, the leaves wither, and soon every tree is bare. The seasons beautifully reveal perfect design and delicate detail. Where there is a design, there must be a Designer.

And think about the glorious heavens. They, more than anything in all creation, declare the absolute majesty of God's power and wisdom. There are billions of stars throughout the heavens. God planted specific planets amidst those stars, and He placed each planet so that it spins perfectly on its axis. Then God specifically chose the planet Earth upon which to build His world. Earth's twenty-four-hour rotation gives us night and day; its precise spin and tilt give us seasons.[4] Without the tilt, we would become a polar ice cap.[5] Earth is the only planet perfectly distanced from the sun and provided with the correct amount of every element needed for life to exist. Earth's atmosphere is perfect to enable us to breathe and to protect us from the sun's deadly heat and rays. God in His wisdom knew that our world had to be just the way it is, placed where it is for you and me to live. He made this world for us to live in and to enjoy!

Then the Lord led me to Psalm 139. For the first time since my rape, a sense of warmth filled my cold, empty heart. As I read the psalmist's words, I realized that God, the Creator of the universe, truly cared about *me*. Look at this psalm with me.

"O Lord, you have examined my heart and know everything about me. You know when I sit or stand. When far away you know my every thought. You chart the path ahead of me, and tell me where to stop and rest. Every moment, you know where I am. You know what I am going to say before I even say it. You both precede and follow me, and place your hand of blessing on my head" (vv. 1–5 TLB).

This Scripture says that God knew every thought I had, understood every emotion I felt, and was interested in every decision I made. It says that He goes behind me and ahead of me. There was never a time that He was not with me. It says that I am alive because God chose to bring me into this world. I have value and infinite worth in His eyes simply because He created me. Even when no one else understands me, my Creator does. In the psalmist's words, I am "fearfully and wonderfully made" (v. 14). God made me; He thought out every part of me. "You made all the delicate, inner parts of my body, and knit them together in my mother's womb. . . . You were there while I was being formed in utter seclusion! You saw me before I was born and scheduled each day of my life before I began to breathe" (vv. 13–16 TLB).

Friend, do you comprehend the significance of these verses? You are not an accident. No matter what anyone has told you, no matter what has happened along your journey, you are valuable to God! You have significance because He created you! Won't you believe God at His Word? Long before you were born, you were conceived in the mind of God. He chose the color of your skin, the texture of your hair, the shape of your body, your talents, and your personality.

Somehow, somewhere deep within me I knew God grieved for me as I suffered at the hands of my rapist.

He placed you in your family. He scheduled every day of your life before you lived out a single day! As I read this psalm repeatedly and soaked up its meaning, I realized that God created me and knows me deeply. He knows my fears, my hurts, my pain, and my humiliation.

Then I read another Scripture that stopped me dead in my tracks. It says that God determined the number of my days and the exact places I would live: "From one man he made every nation . . . and he determined the times set for them and the exact places where they should live" (Acts 17:26). I was confused. If He schedules every day of my life and knows the exact places I will live, then He placed me in that apartment in Waco, Texas. He knew that on June 7, 1986, I would suffer for hours at the hands of a rapist. *How could this be on God's schedule? Why would He plan this event?*

The more I read, the more questions I had. Again, I felt compelled to discover the answers. Part of me was scared of what God would reveal next. Yet, the other part of me was desperate for answers. My search ultimately led me to God's greatest character trait of all: His love. The Bible plainly says that "God is love" (1 John 4:16). Love is the essence of His being. Isaiah 46:4 promises, "Even to your old age and gray hairs I am he, I am he who will sustain you. I have made you and I will carry you; I will sustain you and I will rescue you." Jeremiah 31:3 promises, "I have loved you with an everlasting love; I have drawn you with loving-kindness." Months after my meeting with Dr. Reynolds, God brought his life verse across my path again: "Neither death nor life, neither angels nor demons, neither the present nor the future, nor any powers, neither height nor depth, nor anything else in all creation, will be able to separate us from the love of God that is in Christ Jesus our Lord" (Romans 8:38–39). However, this time it had more meaning because I knew more about God. I knew in my heart that God was telling me that in the midst of my doubts and fears, He loved me. These verses promised there was nothing I could do and nothing that could be done to me that could change that truth. God's Word told me that it was absolutely impossible to get beyond His reach and His unconditional love.

I found the greatest evidence of God's love in a familiar verse that I had seen flashed on the television screen hundreds of times during the Dallas Cowboy games I watched as a child: "For God so loved the world that he gave his one and only Son, that whoever believes in him shall not perish but have eternal life" (John 3:16). God is huge, and we are small. He is holy, and we are sinful. Yet He loved you and me enough to sacrifice the life of His only Son so that we could spend eternity with Him. I was beginning to grasp the wonder of this amazing love. King David recognizes it in Psalm 8:3–5: "When I consider your heavens, the work of your fingers, the moon and the stars, which you have set in place, what is man that you are mindful of him, the son of man that you care for him? You made him a little lower than the heavenly beings and crowned him with glory and honor." The depth of this love He freely gives is truly incomprehensible.

Yes, I grew up knowing Jesus loved me and died for my sins.

We celebrated it every Easter by going to Mass and out to brunch afterward. But that gift, that sacrifice, took on new meaning for me. In one of the books given to me after my attack, I found this wonderful quote by Billy Graham: "That love was for you and for me. The cross exemplified the love of God. . . . The condemnation of God that was borne by Christ was ours. The judgment of God upon sin was ours. The shame of the cross was rightfully ours. But God loved, and God gave His Son."[6] Can you see how God was drawing me closer and closer to Himself, revealing His character bit by bit? He wanted me to take a leap of faith and trust Him with my broken and fearful heart.

I physically felt part of my anger against God subside. It broke my heart as I thought of how God must have suffered as He watched the soldiers lay Jesus on the cross and pound the nails into His hands. How God must have grieved as His one and only Son hung on the cross . . . somehow, somewhere deep within me I knew God grieved for me as I suffered at the hands of my rapist. How could He do any less? Like Jesus, I am God's child, created in His image.

God was changing my perspective in baby steps. Until my meeting with President Reynolds, I had never deeply read my Bible. Now I read with this new perspective of God . . . as sovereign, wise, and loving. More than that, I found myself *desiring* to read His Word, excited to see what God would reveal next.

I began to *know* God more fully. New revelations about my God poured forth from the pages of Scripture. God is *El Shaddai/All Sufficient* (2 Corinthians 12:9–10); the *Alpha and the Omega* (Revelation 21:6); *Counselor* (John 14:26; Isaiah 9:6); *Deliverer* (Psalm 18:2); *Our Hope* (Colossians 1:27); *Bread of Life* (John 6:48); *Shield* (Psalm 91:4); *Strong Tower* (Psalm 61:3); *Provider* (Philippians 4:19); *Judge* (Acts 17:31); *Light of the World* (John 9:5); *Prince of Peace* (Isaiah 9:6), and *Redeemer* (Psalm 19:14; Isaiah 44:6).

Best of all, He wanted to be all of these for me.

I felt hopeless and alone and needed hope. I was in a living hell and needed a Deliverer. I was terrified of the dark and needed light. I was anxious and needed peace. His Word promised He was all of these things and more for me. Do you need any of these in your life? Do you long for delivery from your anguish and pain? Do you long to escape from your prison of darkness? Are you desperate for hope in the midst of your hopelessness? Open His Word. Sit at His feet and ask Him to reveal Himself to you.

Please hear me. The revelations described in this chapter did not happen overnight or in one reading of the Bible. Months or even years passed since the events about which I am writing. Like growing a friendship, growing in the wisdom and knowledge of God takes time. It is a journey. It is a commitment. Your first step is to open God's Word. You may find numerous other philosophies and theories claiming to be truth, but what I pray you will know and believe by the end of this book is that there is only one Truth, and that Truth is God's Word.

When we open His Word, God promises to open our hearts and minds to what it says. There were many times when I opened my Bible and felt nothing. There were other times when I did not understand what I was reading. All God asked of me was that I read it. In His time, He gave me all I needed to know. Trust Him that in His time, He will do the same for you.

The writer of Psalm 119:73 prays, "Your hands made me and formed me; give me understanding to learn your commands." Be patient, my friend. Do not get discouraged if you feel He is not answering your questions or speaking to your situation. He will. Trust Him in the wait. He *is* at work.

CHAPTER THREE

God's Story UNFOLDS

The unfolding of your words gives light; it gives understanding to the simple.

—PSALM 119:130

MONTY AND I WERE the first of our friends to marry, so everyone was excited about our upcoming nuptials. Everyone except me. There were times when I wondered if I should even get married. *What kind of wife would I be?*

Planning my wedding should have been the most wonderful time of my life, but I struggled to survive each day. Simple tasks like waking up, getting dressed, and getting from one place to another took every ounce of my energy. Even though I had moved to a new apartment, I lived in constant fear of my attacker. I looked for him around every corner. I could never enter an empty house alone. I made whoever was with me search every closet, look under every bed, behind every door, and even in the washer and dryer. Memories of the rape invaded my mind at the most unexpected times. Sometimes there were triggers . . . a man with blue eyes, a scene in a movie, a news story, the mention of the word *rape*. Other times, they arrived for no reason at all. When the memories flooded my mind, my body trembled, my heart raced, and I wept uncontrollably. Because I could not sleep, I lived in a state of physical and mental exhaustion. My life was an emotional roller coaster. My volatile state affected everyone around me.

The week before our wedding was a lot of fun. Being surrounded by friends and family meant I was never alone. Showers, brunches, and luncheons filled my days. Parties, spontaneous visits, and family gatherings filled the nights. Love and laughter lit up my life for the first time in a long time.

Finally, the day arrived, May 9, 1987. In the presence of friends and family, we promised to love, honor, and cherish each other until death parted us. It was a beautiful wedding; I truly enjoyed the day! The honeymoon was wonderful and difficult at the same time as we dealt with so many issues stemming from my rape. Monty, as always, was patient and supportive. However, I had trouble *feeling* any kind of love. In the deepest parts of my heart, I wondered if I knew how to love anymore.

I felt better for the moment, but soon my anxious thoughts and fears returned.

Upon returning from our honeymoon, we moved into our new apartment in Dallas. I thought moving to a new city and making a fresh start would make everything better. I soon realized that my pain and fear ran so deep that location made no difference.

Monty and I attended a large church in Highland Park that had many young couples our age. We faithfully attended worship and Sunday school. Eventually, Monty and I bravely tackled teaching middle-school tweens. I joined the Dallas Junior League and volunteered at the Dallas Children's Advocacy Center. One year after we moved to Dallas, I embarked on an intense three-year study of law at Southern Methodist University (SMU). While in law school, I made law review, was a leader within the law school community, interned with some of the top firms in Dallas, and graduated in the top 10 percent of my class.

From the outside looking in, life seemed perfect. However, on the inside, I was crumbling.

I never went anywhere without Monty or a trusted girlfriend. I refused to be alone with any man, even those I knew well. Nightmares continued to plague my sleep. I regularly suffered from panic attacks, several of which landed me in the emergency room. I was exhausted. Living life was such an effort. I desperately wanted to stop being tired, to stop feeling sick, and to live free from controlling fear. I vividly remember early one morning, long before the sun peeked over the horizon, sitting curled up in a ball on my living room floor, shaking my fist at God. *Why did You do this to me? I cannot live like this anymore!*

I continued to pick up my Bible, mostly in my darkest times. It was not daily or even weekly, just when I reached that point of total exhaustion and hopelessness and needed something beyond myself. Each time I opened His Word, God faithfully provided words of peace, comfort, and encouragement. But those feelings never stayed long. I felt better in the moment, but soon my anxious thoughts and fears returned.

A few years after we joined our church, they hired a new minister. One of Pastor Craig's first sermons was on how God speaks to us today through the Scriptures. Quoting John 10:27, he said that God's children hear and know God's voice like sheep know and hear the voice of their shepherd. Jesus says, "My sheep listen to my voice; I know them, and they follow me."

Pastor Craig explained that in Jesus' day, a shepherd had a personal relationship with his sheep. They depended on him daily for survival. The shepherd led his sheep to the greenest pastures and to the purest water. He protected them through the most treacherous of nights. When the shepherd called his sheep, they recognized his voice and followed him like baby chicks follow a mother hen. They knew and trusted their shepherd's voice. Pastor Craig explained that God's voice is God's Word, and today we find God's Word in the Bible. He said that if we allow Him, God will speak to us through His Word.

I could not believe what I was hearing. According to Pastor Craig, I should be able to hear God speak to me as I read the Bible. For me, this was a difficult concept because I saw the Bible as a book written long ago when life was extremely different from ours. I viewed it more like a history book full of interesting stories that contained great life lessons. Yes, in the last few years, God had revealed new ideas to me about His character, but I had never heard Him speak, not even a whisper. I wanted to believe what Pastor Craig said and trust the Bible for more. I longed to find something, anything, that would change my circumstances. I had tried so many things: self-help books, prescription medication, counselors, and well-meaning advice. None worked.

However, inspired by Pastor Craig's sermon, I decided to go to my Bible again, this time specifically listening for God's voice. I came across Isaiah 55:2—"Why spend your money on food that does not give you strength? Why pay for food that does you no good? Listen to me, and you will eat what is good. You will enjoy the finest food" (NLT). Another translation says, "Your soul will delight in the richest of fare." Here was the word *listening* again. *Okay, God, You have my attention. I am listening.*

This verse spoke as if my soul were alive. Moreover, it said my soul would *delight* in listening to God's Word. Up to that point, the only truth I knew about my soul came from a prayer I recited as a small child before bed: *Now I lay me down to sleep, I pray the Lord my soul to keep. If I die before I wake, I pray the Lord my soul to take.* I knew that my soul would go to heaven when I died. I could not comprehend how my soul could delight in anything. After all, I could not touch, feel, or see it.

According to this verse, my alive soul could experience God. The more I studied, I learned that God created my soul and placed it deep within my heart. He intended it to be a place that only He could satisfy. At that point, my soul was a dark, dank, empty place filled with fear and pain. I desperately wanted my soul to be satisfied and filled with the things of God.

Desiring more of God, I studied His Word every chance I got. Deuteronomy 8:3 says that a person lives by "every *word* that comes from the mouth of the Lord." I located the concordance in the back of my Bible and looked up *word*. I found the following Scriptures: "Your *word* is a lamp to my feet and a light for my path" (Psalm 119:105). "The unfolding of your *words* gives light; it gives understanding to the simple" (Psalm 119:130). Reading these verses reminded me of the time I agreed to watch our new neighbors' dog while they were out of town. They left late in the afternoon, so when I went to let the dog out, it was dark. The house was pitch black inside. Being unfamiliar with the layout of the room, I could not locate the light switch in the dark. I stumbled around, tripping over furniture. When I bumped into an end table, I ran my hand across the table until I felt a lamp. The moment I flicked the switch, everything, of course, became visible.

God wanted to use His Word to reach into the depths of my soul and penetrate my heart. That frightened me. . . .

That is how I felt about my life, like I was stumbling around in complete darkness. I had no order, no direction, and no clarity. Sometimes I could barely make it through a day. What saddened me most was that I had no idea how to stop the cycle. If these verses were true and God's Word really was a lamp for my life, maybe this was my answer, the answer I had been searching for these last few years.

I decided to forge on in my attempt at listening for God. I trusted that He wanted me to take the words and stories in His story and allow them to change my life, to speak to my soul. I was not sure how that was supposed to happen, but it became clear He was leading me in that direction when I came across Hebrews 4:12: "For the word of God is living and active. Sharper than any double-edged sword, it penetrates even to dividing soul and spirit, joints and marrow; it judges the thoughts and attitudes of the heart." This verse describes God's Word as living. By living, He means it is relevant to my life today. It is not a dead piece of literature to be read, enjoyed, and put aside. His Word is inexhaustible, meaning that no amount of study can exhaust its potential to work in my life. God's Word is not just a good read; God intended for it to seize my heart and my conscience, to move me and change me.

Hebrews 4 also defines God's Word as *active.* The King James translation uses the word *powerful. Active* means "causing activity or change, capable of exerting influence."[1] God intended for His Word to influence my life and change it for the better. As I continued to soak up many rich stories within the Bible, I came to see the truth of this verse. I saw that His Word, when spoken, convicted people of their sin, converted their hearts, raised the dead to life, and made the deaf to hear, the blind to see, the mute to speak, and the lame to walk.

Another powerful teaching is that His Word is "sharper than any double-edged sword," penetrating "even to dividing soul and spirit, joints and marrow." Here again was another reference to my soul. God wanted to use His Word to reach into the depths of my soul and penetrate my heart. That frightened me because I knew what He would find. Deeply embedded in the soil of my heart were fear, shame, bitterness, and despair. I was afraid to go there, to face the fear, the shame, the anger, and the bitterness. Those feelings and emotions had become one with me; I did not want to confront them. Yet something within me knew I had no choice.

Little by little I began to believe that maybe this Book could answer my questions. Yet a part of me still hesitated. How did I know that these stories were true and could really change *me?* Perhaps the lives of people in the stories changed because they were actually there with God and with Jesus. He walked among them.

He touched them and spoke to them personally. Would He do the same for me?

Demonstrating His faithfulness, God answered my questions as He again led me through His Word. I read my Bible often. My best times with God were early in the morning. As Monty slept, I would curl up in a cozy chair on the sun porch of our first house. One morning God led me to a verse that states clearly that the Bible is the actual Word of God. God inspired the men who wrote it: "All Scripture is God-breathed and is useful for teaching, rebuking, correcting and training in righteousness, so that the man of God may be thoroughly equipped for every good work" (2 Timothy 3:16–17). It says *all Scripture*, not some, not just the New Testament, not just the Old Testament, but *ALL* Scripture. It uses the words *God-breathed*. The very breath of God spoke the words. God was the sole inspiration for every single word on every single page. The men who wrote used neither their own thoughts nor their own words. They wrote only what they received from the Lord.

Intrigued by this discovery, I sought out other verses that reinforced this truth:

"As for God, his way is perfect; the word of the Lord is flawless" (2 Samuel 22:31; see also Proverbs 30:5). "Heaven and earth will pass away, but my words will never pass away" (Matthew 24:35). "The word of the Lord stands forever (1 Peter 1:25). "Your word, O Lord, is eternal; it stands firm in the heavens. Your faithfulness continues through all generations; you established the earth, and it endures. Your laws endure to this day, for all things serve you" (Psalm 119:89–91).

God had earned my trust thus far. The precise order that He had revealed verses to me and the amazing way He answered my questions before I ever verbalized them assured me that His Word is living, active, authentic, and reliable. I had lived for several years in hopelessness and uncertainty; it was comforting to find an absolute, unchanging standard to which I could look for answers.

When I began my three-year study of law at SMU, it was

difficult to find time to read my Bible, but I continued to go to God's Word when I had the time. When Monty was out of town and I was alone, sometimes God's Word was a distraction from my fears, but other times it truly was a comfort. I remember one evening in particular. Monty took a trip to Houston, and I stayed with a friend. As I struggled to fall asleep, I opened my Bible to one of the Gospels. I planned to read a few chapters until I became tired enough to fall asleep. However, I could not stop reading. I moved from one story to another about Jesus' life. I was particularly awed by Jesus' disciples. These men were living, breathing examples of the power of God's Word to change a life, or, in this case, twelve lives. Each of them gave up his family, career, and all that was familiar, safe, and comfortable to follow Jesus, the living Word of God.

Peter, Andrew, James, and John were hardworking fishermen. Yet upon meeting Jesus, James and John abandoned their father and the family business. They risked all they had to venture out into the unknown with a man they barely knew. It was the same story for each of the other disciples. They all dropped everything to follow Jesus, no questions asked. I was amazed that these men willingly devoted three years of their lives following Him wherever He went, often at great risk.

A few weeks after that trip, Monty had to go out of town again, and a friend came to stay with me. Since I was still unable to be alone at night, my friends lovingly took turns being available for me when he traveled. That night, I could not sleep at all. Continuing my reading of the gospel I had begun earlier, I jumped to the end of the story. I found the disciples in the upper room with Jesus celebrating the Last Supper during Passover, unaware of what the next day would bring. Jesus then invited them to accompany Him to the garden of Gethsemane. He walked and talked with them every step of the way, imparting wisdom and clues as to what was about to happen. When they arrived at the garden, He showed the disciples where to stay while He prayed, and took James, John, and

Peter to keep watch with Him. Soon He was arrested, and the disciples could hardly take in His being crucified. No glamour, no glory. Their teacher, their hero, died the death of a common criminal. I can only imagine their feelings. Their actions following His death gave me a glimpse.

The same men—except Judas—who had faithfully followed Jesus for three years, had witnessed all of His miracles, and had heard the entirety of His teachings, now deeply mourned the loss of their beloved teacher and friend. They hid and met in secret, living in constant fear that the Jews would prosecute them for their association with Jesus.

Then suddenly, in the midst of their grief and hopelessness, Jesus appeared. The man whose crucifixion multitudes had witnessed three days before was now standing in front of them very much alive. He opened His hands, and they saw the nail-pierced scars. He lifted His tunic, and they saw His spear-pierced side. He had the same voice and the same countenance as before His death. He performed many miraculous signs to prove to them that it was truly He. It must have been surreal to have seen Jesus hanging on a cross just days before and now to have Him alive and walking among them.

As Jesus Christ visited with His beloved disciples, He gave them a calling, a plan, and a purpose for their future. Luke writes, "This is what is written: The Christ will suffer and rise from the dead on the third day, and repentance and forgiveness of sins will be preached in his name to all nations, beginning at Jerusalem. You are witnesses of these things" (Luke 24:46–47). The disciples were aware that they were the called. They were to be the ones preaching His name to all nations. Jesus then commissioned them to go into all the world and preach the good news.

In addition to His words of commission, Jesus empowered them to accomplish this monumental task by sending His Holy Spirit and baptizing them with His Spirit. In Acts, Jesus says, "John baptized with water, but in just a few days you will be baptized with the Holy Spirit" (Acts 1:5 NLT). Soon after receiving the promised Holy Spirit, the disciples came out of hiding and boldly preached the gospel to all who would listen. They willingly endured physical hardship, poverty, ostracism, prison, and even, for many of them, death.

Do you think these ordinary men would have martyred themselves for a man who was merely a great teacher? Jesus Christ transformed every one of them. They knew that He was much more than a man. They knew He was Emmanuel, God who walked with them in the form of a man. The disciples walked with Jesus as a living, breathing human being. He was with them day in and day out to encourage them, empower them, pray for them, and teach them. Nothing I had read thus far encouraged me as much as the story of these twelve incredible men.

Though I was becoming more comfortable with my Bible, I still had little confidence when I read. Unless it was a simple story, I struggled understanding what God was saying. However, I discovered that Scripture backs up Scripture over and over again. It is as if God knows we need to hear the same Truth many times in many ways to understand it. The more a person reads, the more he or she will understand God's Truths.

What hope this gave me! God wanted to heal me.

For example, Scripture says Jesus Christ is the Word of God made flesh. John writes, "In the beginning was the Word, and the Word was with God, and the Word was God. He was with God in the beginning. . . . The Word became flesh and made his dwelling among us. We have seen his glory, the glory of the One and Only, who came from the Father, full of grace and truth" (John 1:1, 14). The first few times I read this passage, it held little meaning. However, the more I immersed myself in His Word, the more it began to make sense. In this passage, John identifies Jesus as God's self-revelation. Jesus, fully God, came to earth and lived as a human being. He chose twelve disciples and walked alongside them. They saw Him. They heard Him. They touched Him. He was God in human form. What I realized, and what I want you to understand, is that you and I have that same Word available to us today. No, He does not walk among us, but we can still hear Him. The pages of the Holy Bible pour forth His words. We do not have to wait to hear it taught from a priest, a minister, or a teacher. We can open our Bible anytime, anywhere, and hear Him speak to us.

Moreover, just as Jesus' disciples received the Holy Spirit to empower them, you and I have that same opportunity to have God's Spirit living in us, empowering us. In Acts 1:8, Jesus speaks these final words: "You will receive power when the Holy Spirit comes on you; and you will be my witnesses in Jerusalem, and in all Judea and Samaria, and to the ends of the earth." John 16:13–14 says, "But when he, the Spirit of truth comes, he will guide you into all truth. He will not speak on his own; he will speak only what he hears, and he will tell you what is yet to come. He will bring glory to me by taking from what is mine and making it known to you." The Spirit of Truth referred to here is the Holy Spirit. What this told me was that I could as readily apply Jesus' promise of power, as did the twelve disciples. Moreover, as evidenced in the lives of the disciples, when I received what the Holy Spirit was fully equipped to give me, the effects would show. Through the power of the Holy Spirit, Jesus promised to make known to me the very same truths that He taught the disciples!

What hope this gave me! No matter my circumstances, no matter my sorrow, God was telling me that I did not have to manage it in my own strength anymore. God wanted to heal me. He wanted to work in and through me so I could be living proof of His existence, just as He did the disciples.

God did not stop unfolding His story there. He spoke words of life to me late one evening when I thought of ending mine. Following in the tradition of many retirees, my grandparents had years earlier moved to Florida. Then it became our family's tradition to spend Christmas with them and then go to Orlando to spend New Year's Eve at Disney World, along with what seemed like millions of other people! My poor husband married into this tradition, much to his dismay. The first Christmas of our marriage, we planned to make the annual pilgrimage to Florida. During the months preceding our visit, I began experiencing quite a bit of anxiety and fear, which led to numerous panic attacks. My doctor prescribed medication; she also required me to wear a Holter monitor, a cardiac device to monitor my heart rate for a month. I had to wear this awkward contraption twenty-four hours a day, even while we were at Disney.

My condition worsened as I obsessed about my health and emotional state. One evening at my grandparents' home, I lay awake in bed, unable to sleep, silently crying. I pleaded with God to help me. My heart swelled with questions: *How can I go on this way? Will I ever be able to be alone? Will I ever be normal? How can I ever have a family when I cannot even take care of myself? Will Monty stay with me if I continue to burden him this way?* Lying there alone with my fear, I suddenly felt void of emotion, completely empty. I was terrified. For the first time I thought maybe it would be better to be dead.

By some miracle, which I now believe was God through His Holy Spirit, I jumped up from my bed and crept into the bathroom. I sat on the floor, opened my Bible, and God put these beautiful verses before my eyes. Again, He was pointing me back to His Word. Beyond its reliability, authenticity, and power, He showed me that His Word has great purpose:

> *"For my thoughts are not your thoughts, neither are your ways my ways," declares the Lord. "As the heavens are higher than the earth, so are my ways higher than your ways and my thoughts than your thoughts. As the rain and the snow come down from heaven, and do not return to it without watering the earth and making it bud and flourish, so that it*

yields seed for the sower and bread for the eater, so is my word that goes out from my mouth: It will not return to me empty, but will accomplish what I desire and achieve the purpose for which I sent it." (Isaiah 55:8–11)

Here again God was telling me that His storybook was not just another piece of literature to read. No, God painted a beautiful picture of what He intended for His Word to accomplish in my life. Just as rain waters the earth and brings forth a harvest, so God intended His Word to pour into my life and accomplish all He had planned for me.

My friend, His promise is clear. God will accomplish His purposes. In addition, according to the following verse from Jeremiah, His ultimate purpose is good. Jeremiah proclaims, "'For I know the plans I have for you,' declares the Lord, 'plans to prosper you and not to harm you, plans to give you a hope and a future'" (29:11). In Romans, His Word promises that "in all things God works for the good of those who love him, who have been called according to his purpose" (Romans 8:28).

What comfort these verses gave me that night! One man's heinous act stole all that was precious and dear in my life. Yet God was telling me that in the midst of my circumstances, He was working it all for my good. So regardless of how I was feeling or what I could see with my physical eyes, He was asking me to *choose* to trust Him at His Word. He was asking me to have faith. God taught me through His Word that faith does not look at circumstances: "Faith is being sure of what we hope for and certain of what we do not see" (Hebrews 11:1). Faith looks to God, hopes in God, and believes in His promises, regardless of our actual circumstances.

What is your first response when everything around you begins to unravel? Do you look for someone to blame? Do you determine in your own mind what steps you need to take to "fix" the situation?

Do you retreat into a shell? Alternatively, do you look to God? Do you go to His Word? Do you pray for understanding?

I knew God was teaching me, unfolding His story to me, and I wholeheartedly believed everything in His Word. Nevertheless, I was not totally convinced that it could free me from the fear that imprisoned me. Then I read this verse: "You are truly my disciples if you remain faithful to my teachings. And you will know the truth, and the truth will set you free" (John 8:31–32 NLT). This is what I desperately wanted . . . to be set free from all that bound me. Clearly, according to this verse, God's Truth, His Word, is the key. It was the one thing I needed to progress toward complete freedom. I knew then that I had to continue on my journey. I chose to trust that He would show me the way.

My friend, what is holding you back? What is going through your mind as you are reading these verses with me? Will you trust God right now? Will you choose to continue on this journey with me, even in your uncertainty, even in your doubts?

CHAPTER FOUR

Treasures in the DARKNESS

I will give you the treasures of darkness, riches stored in secret places, so that you may know that I am the Lord, the God of Israel, who summons you by name.

—ISAIAH 45:3

I WAS IN MY SECOND year of law school. About midyear my criminal law professor taught a class on the use of DNA testing in criminal investigations. He explained new technology that allowed police to identify perpetrators by body fluids retrieved from the scene of a crime. My thoughts wandered to my humiliating exam at the hospital where they recovered physical evidence from the rapist. Hope filled my heart. I talked to my professor, and he suggested that I contact the police to see if they had recovered evidence that may contain DNA. The next day I contacted the Waco Police Department. The woman I spoke with took my information and said she would have someone return my call.

The wait was agonizing. In my heart, I knew this was it: the answer to all my problems. God was finally going to make everything right. They would test the semen, identify the rapist, punish the rapist, and I would be free.

The next day an officer returned my call. His words cut to my core: "I'm sorry, ma'am, we cannot locate your evidence." *What? How could this be? Surely he's mistaken.* I was speechless. When I could finally focus, fury rose within me. I could not accept his answer. I begged Monty to drive me to Waco; I wanted to talk to someone face-to-face. *Perhaps they did not do a thorough search. If we were there, they would try harder or do more.* Ever supportive, Monty drove me to Waco. When we arrived at the police department, we met with an investigator. He informed us of police routine: once a case is closed, the investigators send the evidence to a remote location where it is stored indefinitely. He then repeated what the officer on the phone told me, "We cannot locate your evidence. It should have been in storage, but it wasn't."

With some hesitation, I decided to give God another chance.

"Where is it then?" I asked.

No one knew. No one had answers. The only fact he could confirm was that the physical evidence from my rape was gone.

His words crushed my dreams for prosecution and retribution. My hope for healing and closure vanished. I cried out to God: *Why are You doing this to me? What have I done to deserve this?* I felt abandoned and alone. No words could comfort me. I again fell into a pit of despair. *How could I go on, knowing he was out there, knowing he would never be punished for what he did to me and what he stole from me?*

Christian friends encouraged me to trust God and have faith that He would use this to work in and through my life. But their words fell on deaf ears. I immediately began to shut out God again. I was so angry with Him. I stopped reading my Bible; I rarely prayed.

But today, I am so thankful for my dear friend Lendy's persistence in continuing to pray for and encourage me. She gave me a book of daily devotionals. Each page included a Scripture at the top followed by an inspirational message from the author related to the verse. The words and Scriptures in the devotions reminded me how God loved me, how He was in control of my life, and how He wanted to speak to me. With some hesitation, I decided to give God another chance. However, I was afraid to trust Him fully; He had let me down. Reluctantly, I began once again to meet God in His Word. It was not long before He brought me back to the word *faith*.

My son, Bo, loves to play baseball. Sometimes I feel as if I spend half my life at the baseball field. In one of his first seasons of playing, the coach put him in at catcher. He loved it so much that he quickly decided that was the position he always wanted to play. I hated it because over the years, I had witnessed the powerful collisions that can happen at home plate. Yet I knew that every boy's dream is to make the big play at home that saves the game.

In the last inning of a very exciting tournament game, I watched the runner from the opposing team round third base and dig in with all he had to cross home plate. As he began to slide, Bo reached high into the air and caught the ball thrown from the outfield. As he brought his glove down, the runner plowed into Bo at full speed in what to me was akin to a full-force football tackle. Bo's small eight-year-old body slammed to the ground. I will never forget the sound that caused my heart to skip a beat and drop into my stomach. I looked at the faces of the mothers around me, and each one reflected deep concern. Bo lay there. I prayed. The coaches surrounded him as he continued to lie still. I prayed for any movement. What seemed an eternity to me was really just a few moments. First Bo's arms moved, then his legs. Finally, he slowly got up.

My first reaction was to run out on that field, pick him up, take him home, and never let him play baseball again. However, because of his love for the sport and his talent at the position, I knew that I had to let go of my fears. I needed to have *faith* . . . *faith* in the coaches to coach him, *faith* in the equipment to protect him, and *faith* in my son to be smart. I grasped that kind of faith, faith based in physical and practical realities. Was the kind of faith that God was asking of me any different? I wanted God to teach me. One of the first verses I read about faith was Hebrews 11:1, which says, "Faith is being sure of what we hope for and certain of what we do not see." Matthew Henry defines *faith* as "a firm persuasion and expectation that God will perform all that He has promised to us in Christ; and this persuasion is so strong that it gives the soul a kind of possession and present fruition of those things, gives them a subsistence in the soul."[1] Up to this point, I thought I had faith. I believed in God. I believed in His Son, Jesus. I believed Jesus died on the cross for me. Moreover, in the last few years, I had come to believe the Bible was the inspired Word of God and that God created me, knew me, and loved me with an everlasting love. But I would not have described my faith as strong. "Strong" faith made me think of spiritual giants like Billy Graham and Mother Teresa, people who devoted their entire lives to serving God. God blessed and honored them with extraordinary treasures because of the calling on their lives.

I wondered if I could ever have a faith like theirs, a deep and abiding faith that trusts God unequivocally. Based on my past record, I did not think so. Then I found another verse that says, "Faith comes from hearing the message, and the message is heard through the word of Christ" (Romans 10:17). If I were honest, I would admit that up to that point, my level of trust in God depended on my circumstances. According to this verse, however, faith comes *not* from circumstances, feelings, or emotions, but from hearing God's Word. In fact, faith has nothing to do with circumstances. Martin Luther wrote, "We must not judge by what we feel or by what we see before us. The Word must be followed and we must firmly hold that these truths are to be believed, not experienced. . . . For the Word must be believed even when we feel and experience what differs entirely from the Word."[2]

I was sure that God was frustrated with me by now. How many times did He have to tell me the same thing? Nevertheless, He was patient. He continued to point me to His Word, where I would find my answers. The burden was on me. I had to take the step of faith and look beyond my circumstances. I had to make a conscious choice to trust Him.

The gospel of Mark, chapter 9, contains a great story about faith. It involves the father of a demon-possessed boy who brings his child to Jesus. The father tells Him that his son has been sick since he was a small child and asks Jesus if he could heal his son (v. 22). Jesus replies, "What do you mean, 'If I can?' . . . Anything is possible if a person believes" (v. 23 NLT). Immediately the boy's father exclaims, "I do believe; help me with my unbelief" (v. 24).

I so identified with that father. He said, "I do believe!" Yet he was honest enough to admit to Jesus that he also had unbelief. His son had been sick for years, and he had prayed many times before for healing. He had even asked the disciples to drive out the spirit, and they failed. His son's circumstances had not changed.

> *Our suffering has a purpose beyond what we see from our limited perspective.*

The father humbly asked Jesus to help him with his unbelief. The Greek word for *unbelief* is *apistols*, meaning "untrustworthy, not worthy of confidence or belief."[3] In truth, the man was not certain Jesus could heal his son. I too wanted to believe God could heal me, but like the father, I was not sure that I fully trusted God. I experienced fleeting moments of trust, but when my evidence disappeared, so too did my trust in Him. Second Corinthians 5:7 (NASB) says, "For we walk by faith, not by sight." Beth Moore writes, "Christ isn't asking us to believe in our ability to exercise unwavering faith. He is asking us to believe He is able."[4] It occurred to me that I was judging God based on what He had done for me lately and not on His character. The crucial bottom line for me was whether I believed God was able to do what His Word promised. Moreover, did I really even know what His Word promised about trials and suffering?

One day while searching through my Bible, I found Isaiah 45:3: "I will give you the treasures of darkness, riches stored in secret places, so that you may *know* that I am the Lord, the God of Israel, who summons you by name." Was this God's answer to my question? Must I first walk through darkness to know God better? Is it in walking through this trial in my life that I would receive His blessings and treasures?

Again, I dug into God's story in search of verses about trials and suffering. I went to my concordance and looked up every verse on suffering. What I discovered was that just because I believed in God and lived a good life did not guarantee I would not experience deep pain and suffering. God's Word, in fact, states the opposite. It plainly says that painful trials *are* a part of God's plan for my life: "Do not be surprised at the painful trial you are suffering, as though something strange were happening to you" (1 Peter 4:12). Page after page of Scripture reveals stories of God's chosen people suffering painful and difficult trials. Adam and Eve, Abraham, David, Joseph, Job, Daniel, Paul, John, and many others endured tremendous hardships and suffering: delayed answers to prayer, unanswered prayer, impossible circumstances, personal challenges, great temptation, persecution, and seemingly senseless tragedies.

Why would God promise this? It seemed cruel. Yet His Word is clear: "Consider it pure joy, my brothers, *whenever* you face trials of many kinds, because you know that the testing of your faith develops perseverance. Perseverance must finish its work so that you may be mature and complete, not lacking anything" (James 1:2–4). Notice it does not say *if* you face trials but *when*. They will come. In Romans 5:3–5, it says we endure suffering "because we know that suffering produces perseverance; perseverance, character; and character, hope. And hope does not disappoint us, because God has poured out his love into our hearts by the Holy Spirit, whom he has given us."

Our suffering has a purpose beyond what we see from our limited perspective. Peter writes: "In this you greatly rejoice, though now for a little while you may have had to suffer grief in all kinds of trials. These have come so that your faith—of greater worth than gold . . . may be proved genuine and may result in praise, glory and honor when Jesus Christ is revealed" (1 Peter 1:6–7). The King James translation reads: "Wherein ye greatly rejoice, *though now for a season, if need be,* ye are in heaviness through manifold temptations: that the trial of your faith, being much more precious than of gold that perisheth, though it be tried with fire, might be found unto praise and honour and glory at the appearing of Jesus Christ" (1 Peter 1:6–7). Notice the words "for a season" and "if need be." Peter tells us that sometimes it is necessary to walk through the fiery trial. Our suffering is not meaningless because God has a plan. He asks us to trust in that plan, and we can because we trust in Him.

This realization brought even more questions: *Why must God do it this way? Isn't there a better way to develop character and maturity?* And in that moment, God brought me a story to teach me this truth . . . a powerful story.

The joy experienced in the birth of a child is unmatched. I sat by the bedside of my friend Lendy as she lay in the hospital, preparing to give birth to her first child. I shared with you earlier that of all the godly influences in my life at that time, Lendy was the greatest. Throughout our four years at Baylor, I watched her walk faithfully with the Lord, never wavering from her commitment despite the pressures she encountered. She daily met with the Lord in prayer and quiet time. Whenever any of us had a problem, we went to Lendy. She would pray with us and always had the perfect verse or truth to share. This was who she was, and everyone around her saw it.

As Lendy's contractions grew stronger, I moved to the waiting room with many other friends and family. A few hours later, the nurse entered and announced that Lendy had given birth to a baby boy. No details, no hugs, not even a smile. She quietly walked out of the room. It was hardly the joyous announcement we had expected. We waited for her husband, Wilson, to come and share details, but he did not come. As time passed, deep concern filled the room. Finally, Wilson did come and told us that doctors believed their son was born with Down Syndrome. They were running tests to confirm the initial diagnosis. Lendy was in her twenties, and this was her first child. It made no sense. *How could this be?* My heart cried out to the Lord: *Not her, Lord, not Your faithful servant.*

I found myself angry with God. Sadly, He must have been used to it by now. I just could not understand how He could allow this in *her* life. Of all my friends, Lendy lived for Him the loudest, in glorious color for all to see. However, as I watched her over the next few weeks and months, it became clear why the Lord allowed this in her life. We all marveled at Lendy's response to news that would have devastated most mothers. Initially, she spent time alone with baby Coleman and with God. She prayed and cared for Coleman with a depth of love that amazed everyone. Her faith never wavered. She never asked, *Why me?* That would have been my first question. Yet Lendy had an incomprehensible peace. She trusted God fully and completely.

How? She believed God at His Word. She trusted that God has a divine purpose for Coleman's life. Coleman's diagnosis caught us by surprise, yet God knew this day would come before Coleman was born. Lendy had prayed for him before he was born, during every day of her pregnancy, and every day since. Because of that, Lendy had peace; she trusted God with His plan and surrendered hers.

Today Coleman is a thriving, active, middle-school boy. Doctors told Lendy and Wilson that Coleman would never play sports. Yet he participates in and enjoys many athletic activities. Coleman interacts well with adults and children alike. He is an incredible big brother to four siblings. His life is a beautiful reflection of the love, care, and prayers his mother and father invested in him over the years.

I have watched Lendy love Coleman, encourage him, discipline him, and fall on her knees before God, trusting Him with every fiber of her being. This storm of suffering was not easy, but it has intensified and increased her faith in Jesus. Francois Fenelon writes, "Faith is being willing to let God act with the most perfect freedom, knowing that we belong to Him and are to be concerned only about being faithful in that which He has given us to do for the moment."[5] Lendy did just this. In the midst of her suffering, she drew closer to God. She set her focus on Him and not on her circumstances. She believed God at His Word. She trusted that God would use this event in her life to accomplish His work.

God compares His work in our suffering to refining precious metals. Zechariah the prophet spoke God's words to the Israelites: "Two-thirds of all the nation of Israel will be cut off and die, but a third will be left in the land. I will bring the third that remain through the fire and make them pure, as gold and silver are refined and purified by fire. They will call upon my name and I will hear them; I will say, 'These are my people,' and they will say, 'The Lord is our God'" (Zechariah 13:8–9 TLB). Another prophet, Malachi, says "For he will be like a refiner's fire. . . . He will sit as a refiner and purifier of silver; he will purify the Levites and refine them like gold and silver" (Malachi 3:2–3). Still another prophet, Jeremiah, says, "Therefore this is what the Lord Almighty says: 'See, I will refine and test them, for what else can I do because of the sin of my people?'"(Jeremiah 9:7).

In ancient times, refiners took crushed ore and heated it in special furnaces to extract the gold and remove all impurities. The refiner knew the gold was pure when he saw his reflection in it. God appointed prophets to warn the Israelites that He would refine them just as a refiner tests metals. So it is with us. God alone knows exactly what you and I must endure in order to form His character in us. It is in our trials that God refines us and removes our impurities. Like refined gold, when we pass through our trials, people will see His perfect reflection in us.

The tough question for us as His children is this: Are we willing to accept His refinement? Even when we choose not to accept it, it happens. Look at what the Lord told the prophet Jeremiah: "I have made you a tester of metals and my people the ore, that you may observe and test their ways. They are all hardened rebels, going about to slander. They are bronze and iron; they all act corruptly. The bellows blow fiercely to burn away the lead with fire, but the refining goes on in vain; the wicked are not purged out. They are called rejected silver, because the Lord has rejected them" (Jeremiah 6:27–30). The choice is ours. We can determine in our hearts not to cooperate with God but to rebel. However, when we choose this path, we endure double suffering. Fighting God guarantees greater and longer pain than if we humble ourselves, submit to His will, and ask Him to help us. We must be willing to wait on Him during times of refinement.

If you are going through a difficult time right now, a time of refinement, trust God's promise that He will work it for good. As Romans 8:28 assures us, "And we know that in all things God works for the good of those who love him, who have been called according to his purpose."

Trusting is particularly difficult when your trial or hardship is due to no fault of your own, such as the death of a child, the loss of a job, or a devastating illness. You so desperately want an answer to "Why me?" You want a tangible reason. Did you do something wrong? Did you not pray hard enough? God wants you to take your questions to Him. It may be that God sees a place in your life that needs refining or transforming, or it may be that you live in a fallen world where bad things happen. The promise you have from God is that He will use the difficult circumstances to perfect you and make you more like Him. David cries out in Psalm 139, "Search me, O God, and know my heart; test me and know my anxious thoughts. Point out anything in me that offends you, and lead me along the path of everlasting life" (vv. 23–24 NLT).

I believed that because I was the victim, I had every right to be angry and bitter. After all, I was innocent. In the beginning that was true: I had been the victim of a terrible crime. However, when

I allowed my victim mentality to consume my life, I moved into disobedience toward God. I should have gone to Him immediately. I should have surrendered my emotions to Him and gone to His Word for healing and direction on how to proceed through my pain and grief. By holding on to the victim mentality, I allowed Satan to use my emotions to keep me from living the full life God desired for me.

You and I have a choice, and choosing to accept our circumstances as they are, letting go of blame (whomever we blame), and seeking God's purpose are always the roads we should take. My dear friend and neighbor Karla chose to do just that. Several years ago, my friend Lisa and I started a Bible study in our neighborhood. We meet at my house every other Friday from September through May, and just over the last five years, we have grown from twelve members to nearly forty. A few years ago, Karla, a sweet young mom moved in next door. She had two little girls, Betsy and Claire, and she was pregnant with her third child when I invited her. After she gave birth to Lilly, she accepted the invitation to join our group. We were studying Linda Dillow's book *Calm My Anxious Heart* that semester. This particular week our lesson focused on suffering. As we went around the circle, each woman shared stories about how she had experienced suffering. When Karla's turn came, she passed and said that she had nothing to share. She admitted that she had trouble finishing her homework because she had no answer for that question. The girls in the circle laughed and told her to be thankful. A few minutes later, her small group leader stopped the lesson, looked directly into Karla's eyes and said, "Karla, I think God is preparing you for something." There was an audible gasp from the group. Her leader quickly added, "I do not think you are going to suffer, but God is preparing you to help someone else who will suffer."

God's peace blanketed her in that emergency room.

Karla called me later that afternoon and shared that since Lisa had spoken those chilling words, she felt sick in the pit of her stomach. Lisa's words frightened her. I encouraged her to pray about it. She did so, and God brought to her mind one particular verse from that week's lesson: "When you go through deep waters, I will be with you. When you go through rivers of difficulty, you will not drown" (Isaiah 43:2a NLT). The key word she saw was *when*, not *if.* Questions came to her mind that she had never thought of: If tragedy comes, how would she react? Would she still be thankful? Would she be able to praise God in the midst? She sensed a need to prepare. So she began to prepare . . . for what she did not know.

Karla read her Bible more during the next two weeks than she ever had before. She prayed and reviewed our lesson many times. Two weeks later to the day, she and her husband, Lin, rushed their six-month-old daughter, Lilly, to the emergency room. The doctors immediately whisked her away to the pediatric ICU. Karla and Lin stood there stunned as the doctor told them their precious Lilly was moments away from a diabetic coma. It had all happened so fast. When they finally saw Lilly, tubes laced her tiny body and an oxygen mask covered her ashen face. Karla thought she would fall apart. Yet she remembers looking into Lilly's eyes and having a peace fall upon her. In that moment, all her fears disappeared, and praises poured forth from her lips. She praised God for getting them to the hospital in time, for the doctor ordering a blood test for no apparent reason, and for the diagnosis of diabetes and not something graver.

God's peace blanketed Karla in that emergency room. She sensed God's presence more powerfully that day than she ever had before. Each day God gave her new strength, strength outside of herself. Baffled, Lin asked how she was coping so well when he felt like his world was falling apart. She journaled this response in a letter to Lilly: *God prepared me for this; He prepared my heart and mind, and I totally surrendered you to Him.* She remembered God's promise to her: "When you go through deep waters, I will be with you. When you go through rivers of difficulty, you will not drown."

Yes, we can read God's great storybook. Yes, we can enjoy the stories. It is only when we believe His Word is Truth and meant for us today that it will become relevant and meaningful in our lives. Karla heard God's Word and believed He was speaking directly to her. She *listened* to God. She pondered what she heard, hid it in her heart, and recalled it when she needed it. If we are not willing to do the same, we will never know God's perspective. We will never grow in our relationship with Him.

God created in each one of us a place in our hearts to need Him. Ecclesiastes 3:11 tells us that God has planted eternity in our hearts, a place that longs for God, and a place that only He can fill. To free up that place for Him, He will allow experiences in our lives that seem unfair, difficult, and sometimes tragic.

The Truth of God's story was coming alive for me.

Often our pain and heartache prohibit God from filling that place with His treasures. We harbor so much negative emotion that we cannot get beyond it. That is what I had been doing. Fear filled my heart. In fact, it seemed as if fear filled my entire being. There was no room for God because I had allowed my fear to paralyze me. God did not give up on me. He put another story, this one from His Word, across my path.

Exodus tells the story of the Israelites escaping from slavery in Egypt. Initially, Pharaoh agreed to let God's people go, but soon after they left, he changed his mind. He began to pursue them with six hundred of his best chariots. As Pharaoh approached, the Israelites were terrified. They cried out to Moses. Moses reminded the people of God's promise that He would deliver them. With their ears, they heard the rumble of the chariots charging toward them. With their eyes, they saw a huge body of water blocking their only means of escape.

Can you imagine their fear? The reality they knew was that

Pharaoh's finest soldiers were pursuing them, and there was a huge obstacle, the Red Sea, preventing their escape. God's people had no idea of the miracle awaiting them. After Moses stretched out his hand over the sea, "All that night the Lord drove the sea back with a strong east wind and turned it into dry land" (Exodus 14:21). Because it was dark, the Israelites could not see what God was doing. In the dark of night, God tirelessly worked on behalf of His children to deliver them, just as He promised.

God used this story to alter my perspective. Although the Israelites could not see or hear God, He was working in the midst of their darkness. I too could not "see" or "feel" God, but He was at work around me in invisible ways through the stories and Scriptures I have shared with you. He was present and active, working on my behalf to carry me through my dark place.

In the dark, we have two choices. We can take matters into our own hands, turning to drugs or alcohol to numb our pain, seeking out doctors, friends, or the latest self-help book, never really knowing if any of them is the way to healing and wholeness. Alternatively, we can look to God. We can open His Word, and in that Word we are guaranteed healing and wholeness. Psalm 119:92 (NLT) says, "If your instructions hadn't sustained me with joy, I would have died in my misery." Psalm 107:20 (NLT) says, "He sent out his word and healed them, snatching them from the door of death."

At times, my darkness seemed to suffocate me. Other times I experienced God in powerful and obvious ways. God in His faithfulness continued pursuing me. The experiences I have shared in this chapter helped me to trust God at His Word even when I could not see Him with my eyes. Every step of the way when I sought an answer, He provided it. When I needed to know He was there, He would reveal Himself through a circumstance, a verse, or a friend. The first few years after my rape, I spent many a night locked in my room reading my Bible, the pages soaked with my tears. I would read the words repeatedly. At the time, they held no meaning. Yet as time passed, God reminded me of those promises. He had planted them in my heart, and they took root. When fear overcame me, I could recall them. Isaiah 45:3 that we read at the beginning of the chapter—"I will give you the treasures of darkness, riches stored in secret places, so that you may know that I am the Lord, the God of Israel, who summons you by name"—is a promise directly from God to you and to me. This verse and the others in this chapter assured me that not only would I survive this trial, but also I would be blessed and strengthened.

The truth of God's story was coming alive for me. I now believed God was worthy of my trust, no matter my circumstances. I believed He desired only good for my life and had treasures waiting for me on the other side of this. Yet, I still lived with the practical realities of my self-imposed prison. Fear and anxiety still controlled my day-to-day life. I continued to have flashbacks; I dreaded being alone; I tensed up every time I saw a man with blue eyes; I refused to be anywhere alone with a man. Practically, I did not know how God's Word could free me from this prison.

On the MAT

What is impossible with men is possible with God.

—LUKE 18:27

WHAT I TRULY DESIRED was a new beginning. I wanted God to remove my fear, my hurt, and my anxiety. I wanted to go back to life the way I lived it before my rape. I wanted a new beginning. However, was that a realistic hope?

As I continued my search for answers, I discovered that God is a God of new beginnings, but not in the way I was thinking. The Bible repeatedly testifies to God's transformational work in and through the lives of His people. The great news is that the people in whose lives He did His most powerful work were not men and women who had it all together. They were more often hurting, doubting, disobedient, fearful, weak people just like me. Isaiah 61:1, 3 says that God sent Jesus to "bind up the brokenhearted, to proclaim freedom for the captives and release from darkness for the prisoners . . . bestow on them a crown of beauty instead of ashes, the oil of gladness instead of mourning, and a garment of praise instead of a spirit of despair." As the pages of Scripture unfolded stories of restoration and transformation, I began to believe that God could take any life, even mine, and totally transform it for His glory.

The apostle Paul provides a great example of the magnificence of God's transforming power. Paul, born Saul, was both a Jew and a Roman citizen. He possessed all status and privileges of a Roman citizen, yet he was trained and skilled in Jewish theology. Because of his heritage and his devotion to Jewish law, Saul relentlessly persecuted the early followers of Jesus. He had as his mission to destroy all believers in Christ.

Despite his zealous persecution of the early church, God appointed the unlikely Saul to be one of the greatest evangelists in the history of Christianity. Why would God do this? First, Saul's background and qualifications suited him eminently for the work to which God was calling him. He knew the Jewish culture and language. Since Saul had grown up in Tarsus, he was familiar with Greek culture and its philosophies, and in addition, was a Roman citizen. Finally, God would use the zeal with which Saul persecuted believers in Jesus to preach the gospel throughout the world.

One day as Saul approached the town of Damascus to capture and imprison Christians, Scripture says a bright light from heaven flashed around him. He fell to the ground and heard a voice asking, "Saul, Saul why do you persecute me?"

Saul asked, "Who are you, Lord?"

The voice replied, "I am Jesus, whom you are persecuting. . . . Now get up and go into the city, and you will be told what you must do" (Acts 9:5–6). The men traveling with Saul were speechless; they heard the sound but saw nothing. When he got up, he opened his eyes but could not see. God had covered his eyes, and he experienced three days of blindness.

Meanwhile in Damascus, by means of a vision God had instructed Ananias, a disciple of Christ, to restore Paul's sight. Knowing Saul's reputation, Ananias expressed his fear. The Lord assured Ananias: "This man is my chosen instrument to carry my name before the Gentiles and their kings and before the people of Israel. I will show them how much he must suffer for my name" (Acts 9:15). Ananias obeyed and sought out Paul within the city. He placed his hands on him and said, "Brother Saul, the Lord—Jesus, who appeared to you on the road as you were coming here—has sent me so that you may see again and be filled with the Holy Spirit" (Acts 9:17). Immediately scales fell from Saul's eyes, and he regained his sight.

"Could I ever be content and at peace?"

What happened to Saul on the road to Damascus radically changed his life. *Radical* may be an understatement. Saul became one of the very believers in Jesus whom he had been persecuting. God changed Saul's name to Paul, and he spent the remainder of his life faithfully proclaiming Jesus as the Son of God. His radical transformation is what gives his testimony so much credibility.

Paul's life as an apostle of Christ was far from easy. He sacrificed everything—family, friends, power, prestige, respect, and political freedom—to follow Christ. He suffered great poverty, endured horrendous beatings, experienced shipwrecks, and spent time under house arrest or in prison. Despite all these difficult circumstances, his letters contain some of the richest and truest words on how to live a life filled with God's peace and contentment, no matter your circumstances.

Paul writes, "Not that I was ever in need, for I have learned how to be content with whatever I have. I know how to live on almost nothing or with everything. I have learned the secret of living in every situation, whether it is with a full stomach or empty, with plenty or little. For I can do everything through Christ who gives me strength" (Philippians 4:11–13 NLT). Paul reveals to the reader that *the secret* of his contentedness comes from his relationship with Jesus Christ. Whatever Paul was facing, he was sustained not by his external circumstances but by the constant supply of strength flowing into Him through the life of Jesus Christ. What utterly amazing words, considering Paul's external circumstances.

Questions flooded my mind again. *Could God transform my life in such an astounding way? Could I ever be content and at peace in the midst of the fear, anger, and despair that plagued my life?* Going back to Paul's words in Philippians, I sat down and dissected the passage verse by verse. I noticed one word in particular: *learned.* Paul writes that he *learned* to be content. It did not come naturally to him. Paul chose contentment by altering his behavior.

Paul's words indicate that his secret was *the person* he knew. The *One* he knew gave him strength in the midst of struggle and turmoil. The *One* he knew was Jesus Christ. Christ was the source of Paul's abiding strength. Jesus personally spoke to him on the road to Damascus. Immediately thereafter, he experienced a life change that he knew only God could bring about.

Although it was long in coming, I finally understood that God in His sovereignty allowed my rape. He did not cause it to happen, but I now believed that it was part of His plan. My comfort came in knowing He had a purpose for it in my life. He promised to use it mightily for His kingdom *if* I would let Him. Welling up within me was a deep desire to allow Him to use me. Yet I was afraid . . . afraid of what that would require of me. However, I could not take a step in that direction until I learned to be content with my life as it was, fears and all. Can knowing God intimately really bring peace, even in the midst of great pain and turmoil? Was Paul's secret applicable to everyone? Let me share with you the story of my friend Karen. Doctors diagnosed her with breast cancer. I remember how nervous I was to see her for the first time following her diagnosis. What would I say? I did not want to be one of those friends who say the wrong thing.

Prayer fixes our thoughts on who God is and on what He can do.

I happened to see Karen one afternoon. I lifted a prayer, asking the Lord to give me the right words. As I hugged her, she stepped back and smiled, and I will never forget what she said. She shared that although it was a difficult time, God had gone before her and prepared the way. Bible verses she memorized as a child, sermons she heard, Bible studies she had done, and hymns she knew had been pouring back into her heart and mind. His promises, His love, and His peace washed over her every day. Joy filled my heart as she enthusiastically shared all that God had been doing in her life since her diagnosis. How ironic—I thought I would be the one to encourage her!

Beginning in her childhood, and continuing in her adulthood, Karen had been growing her relationship with God. She was in constant communion with Him through prayer and study. Karen *knew* God. Now when she needed Him, He poured His strength into her to provide all she needed to survive breast cancer as a victor, not a victim. Her faith gave her a supernatural peace that carried her through.

Paul, in his writings, provides systematic directions on how to obtain that peace and contentment. He writes, "Don't worry about anything; instead, pray about everything. Tell God what you need and thank him for all he has done. Then you will experience God's peace, which exceeds anything we can understand. His peace will guard your hearts and minds as you live in Christ Jesus" (Philippians 4:6–7 NLT). This is not a suggestion; it is a command. *Anxiety* comes from the Greek word *merimna*. It stems from the word *merizo*, which means "to draw in different directions, to distract."[1] *Merimna* signifies something that causes an anxious care. Anxiety divides our mind and distracts us from our relationship with God. It is self-centered and counterproductive. It causes us to fix our eyes on our circumstances rather than on God. Anxiety occurs when worry becomes the dominating factor in our lives. Proverbs 12:25 says, "An anxious heart weighs a man down." Jesus Himself asks, "Who of you by worrying can add a single hour to his life?" (Matthew 6:27).

Prayer, on the other hand, is God-centered. Prayer fixes our thoughts on who God is and on what He can do. It draws us away from our worries and presses us closer to the heart of God. We have confidence to pray because we know the One to whom we pray is sovereign, wise, and in control of every detail of our lives. In John 16:33, Jesus reminds us that, "I have told you these things, so that in me you may have peace. In this world you will have trouble. But take heart! I have overcome the world."

Anxiety and prayer are opposing forces that cannot coexist. They cause a battle in our minds, and one will always win out over the other. It is up to us to choose which one will govern our lives. Will we choose to fix our eyes on our troubles or fix our eyes on God? Fixing our eyes on God means we are not to worry about *anything*. Paul tells us that no matter what it is, big or small, we must not worry. That was important for me to hear because I wondered if Paul's *anything* included my fear. What I discovered was that anything does mean anything. Anything that divides my mind and pulls my thoughts away from trusting in God is included in God's command. From experience, I knew that if I let in one worry or one fear, a plethora of both would follow.

God's alternative to being anxious for nothing is to pray about everything. Once again, the word is *everything*. Everything means everything, whether big or small, significant or insignificant. Why prayer? Because in prayer we no longer magnify our problem, we magnify God. However, it is our choice; we must *choose* to give everything over to God.

My choice thus far had been fear. I spent my days ensuring that I was never alone . . . especially with men. From the time I woke up, I planned my day with that in mind. I showered only when I knew Monty or a friend would be home. I never got on an elevator unless there was a woman with me. If we rode a few floors and the woman got off, leaving me alone with a man, I would get off and try again. As a young associate in a law firm, I worked mostly with men. I went to great lengths to protect myself from ever being alone with any of them. I only met clients in public places. I never rode alone in a car with a man. While some of the precautions I took are common sense for any woman, I was inconveniencing anyone and everyone to protect myself. Do you get the picture? I had to be in total control at all times. This caused me to be in a constant state of anxiety. I desperately wanted and needed Paul's words to become a reality in my life.

I did pray and ask God to take my fear away. I honestly believed I was doing what God required of me to receive His peace. Yet, day after day, I remained afraid. I continued to manipulate my life and others' lives to ensure my security and peace of mind. I could not understand what I was doing wrong. Were my prayers not good enough for God?

I went back and examined Philippians 4:6–7 further. Paul finishes this prescription for worry by telling us to thank God for His answers. Am I to be thankful for worries, for suffering, and for tragedies? I did not understand what God was asking. How can people be thankful under such circumstances? How can parents be thankful as they bury a child? How can a couple be thankful when they cannot have a child? How can a wife be thankful when her husband has an affair? How can a woman be thankful when hearing the words "breast cancer"? For my personal situation, it seemed God was asking me to be thankful for my rape.

These were all powerful and encouraging words, but I had no clue how to live them.

As I studied more, I came to understand that God was not asking me to give thanks for the circumstances themselves. He was asking me to focus on what He was doing in my life in the midst of my circumstances. Karen, in the midst of her breast cancer, received cards, e-mails, and phone calls daily to encourage her. There were days when she was totally exhausted and physically sick from the chemotherapy, and she wanted to give up. It was in those moments that God faithfully provided a word of encouragement. He used her friends to remind her of His love for her and His faithfulness. Her response? A heart filled with thanksgiving.

Karla's story echoes the same message. When she felt she could not take another step and believed Lilly's diagnosis was too much to bear, friends flooded their home with cards, meals, and offers to babysit. One friend came and cleaned her entire home while she was away. Coincidence? Absolutely not. God knew what Karla needed in the moment, and in His faithfulness, He provided.

Karla's response? Overwhelming thankfulness, even in the midst of her pain and sorrow.

When we are anxious for nothing and pray about everything, Paul writes that we "will experience God's peace, which exceeds anything we can understand" (Philippians 4:7 NLT). It is a God-given promise. What we receive is not a state-of-mind kind of peace, but a deep, abiding peace, an inner tranquility . . . not the peace the world gives, but a peace that only comes through knowing Jesus Christ as our Lord and Savior and trusting Him. In his gospel, John quotes Jesus: "Peace I leave with you; my peace I give you. I do not give to you as the world gives. Do not let your hearts be troubled and do not be afraid" (John 14:27). It extends to the very core of our being. We know we belong to God and our life is in His hands. He is in control. Elisabeth Elliot describes it this way: "Peace does not dwell in outward things, but in the heart prepared to wait trustfully and quietly on Him who has all things safely in His hands."[2] Jesus specifically uses the words "do not be afraid" in this verse. He was speaking to me!

Paul further writes that God's peace *keeps* or *guards* our hearts and minds. A guard is one who stands watch over something or someone, protecting it with his life. When I read this verse, I pictured angels encamped around my heart, protecting me from the fear and anxiety battling for my mind.

These were all powerful and encouraging words, but I had no clue how to live them. But I persevered. Paul completed His instructions in the next verse: "Finally, brothers, whatever is true, whatever is noble, whatever is right, whatever is pure, whatever is lovely, whatever is admirable—if anything be excellent or praise-worthy—think about such things" (Philippians 4:8). Simply stated, Paul's words were telling me that whatever I put into my mind determined what would come out in my thoughts, words, and actions. Consequently, it was critical that I examine the thoughts that occupied my mind. What was I inputting? I was constantly inputting fear. Thus every thought I had, every word I spoke, and every action I took reflected that message. I was not thinking on what Paul was telling me to think on—that which is pure, true, admirable, excellent, and praiseworthy. I was obsessed with my external circumstances. Paul's message to me was that if I continued to allow my circumstances to dictate my contentedness, I would never be content.

Practically, how was I to change my thoughts? It seemed clear to me that I had to dwell on God's Word and His promises. Paul directs in 2 Corinthians 10:5 to "demolish arguments and every pretension that sets itself up against the knowledge of God, and we take captive every thought to make it obedient to Christ." Satan desired to steal my peace. He wanted me to continue to live bound up in fear. He was filling my thoughts with doubts, worries, irrational fears, and accusations. God desired to give me peace. He wanted to fill my mind with truth, assurance, wisdom, encouragement, and hope. I had to choose to stop listening to Satan's lies. I had to rid my heart and my mind of all the negative thoughts and choose to bow to the truth of God's Word. The only way to do this was to take captive my every thought. Each time fear entered my mind, I had to capture it and replace it with a Scripture, a prayer, or some other godly inspiration. Paul's promise assured me that as I took my thoughts captive, fear and anxiety would lose their hold on me.

You and I are responsible for choosing obedience, for casting out all negative thoughts, and for dwelling on the positive. However,

I want to be clear: This does not mean that we will never have a negative thought again. It does mean that we recognize the thought and answer it with the Word of God. We strip the thought of its power over us as we put it up against Scripture.

We can do this in many ways. First, meditate on who God is: *Shield* (Psalm 119:114; Psalm 3:3) and *Defender* (Proverbs 23:11), *Savior* (1 Timothy 4:10) and *Redeemer* (Psalm 19:14), *Faithful and True* (Revelation 19:11), *All Powerful* (2 Corinthians 4:7), *King of kings and Lord of lords* (1 Timothy 6:15). As we meditate, we are training our minds to think on the character of God. This reassures us that the One to whom we are giving our thoughts is the One in whom we can trust.

Second, search the Scriptures for verses that speak to your particular negative thoughts. Write the verses on note cards or sticky notes and place them in your Bible, throughout your house, in your office, and in your car. Memorize them so that when your fear or worry comes, you can speak the truth God has given you. You replace the lie with truth. This is a long process and requires that we be diligent and prayerful. Just like changing eating habits or exercise habits, it requires discipline. The hardest part is taking the first step.

My first big victory comes in this part of my story. God gave me 2 Timothy 1:7—"For God has not given us a spirit of fear and timidity, but of power, love, and self-discipline" (NLT). I knew I had choices to make, and I knew God's Word taught me how to make them. I just had not taken the steps to obey. I was praying and asking God for wisdom. We were still living in Dallas and attending Highland Park United Methodist Church. One Sunday our senior minister, Mark Craig, preached a sermon that touched me deeply. Strangely, today I cannot remember the topic of the sermon. I now believe it was God's way to get me into his office. As much as I wanted an appointment, I thought in a church with over ten thousand members that I did not have a good chance of getting to see him, at least anytime soon. Still, I called his office. His secretary took my name and number. That afternoon, he personally called me and scheduled a visit later that week.

As I entered the building, my stomach churned. I did not know specifically why I was there. His words had touched me, but now that I was meeting him, I did not know what to say.

Pastor Craig greeted me and invited me into his office. It brought back memories of my "God appointment" with Dr. Reynolds many years before. As soon as I sat down, Pastor Craig smiled and inquired about the purpose of my visit. Much to my surprise, I poured out my entire story. I shared with him what I had been through and told him of the fears that gripped my life. The words flowed even though he was a complete stranger. As I was talking, he interrupted and asked if I had ever read the story of the invalid in the gospel of John. I said that it was a vague memory. He suggested that we read the story together. I clumsily flipped through the New Testament. With a little help, I found John 5 and began to read.

Pastor Craig asked, "Wendy, do you want to get well?"

John writes of a man who had been an invalid for thirty-eight years. For many of those years, he sat at the edge of a pool where a great number of blind, lame, and paralyzed people came, hoping to be healed. The people of that time believed that once a day an angel would come down to the water and stir it. The people believed that healing powers entered the pool the moment the angel touched it. Whoever touched the water first after the stirring would be healed. When Jesus saw the invalid lying there, He asked him, "Do you want to get well?"

At those words, I stopped reading, looked at my minister and without thinking exclaimed, "What a stupid question!" I quickly realized that I had just told our minister, whom I had never met before that day, that Jesus asked a stupid question. A wave of nausea overcame me, and I was afraid of what he would say. He simply smiled and asked me to continue. "'Sir,' the invalid replied, 'I have no one to help me into the pool when the water is stirred. While I am trying to get in, someone else goes down ahead of me.' Then Jesus said to him, 'Get up! Pick up your mat and walk.' At once the man was cured; he picked up his mat and walked" (John 5:6–9).

When I finished reading, Pastor Craig looked deep into my eyes and asked, "Wendy, do you want to get well?" This time, although I thought it, I restrained from repeating *what a stupid question.* I responded with what I believed to be my honest answer, "Of course I want to get well."

He gently said, "I really don't think that you do."

Pastor Craig told me that I was like that invalid. My fear had paralyzed me, and I lived in a prison of fear and self-pity that I had created. The frank words he spoke hit me hard. For years, I had remained in my place of pain, sorrow, lack of forgiveness, and fear. I had settled there. Worse, a man who barely knew me accused me of being comfortable there.

"God has so much more for your life," Pastor Craig explained. He said that Christ died on the cross to give me a new life, an abundant life. It was not until I had the courage to get up and walk that I would ever know that abundant life. He prayed with me and challenged me to pray about my next step.

My meeting with Mark Craig was another "God appointment," used to teach me a powerful truth about His Word. What seemed such a simple Bible story truly came alive that day in the pastor's office. God, the Master Storyteller, spoke loudly and clearly. Scripture says that God sent His Word to guide, teach, rebuke, and discipline. That day, I received God's rebuke. It was a hard truth to hear, but it was time for me to choose. Would I listen and obey? Would I get up from my mat of despair, take God's hand, and walk with Him?

I decided to take some drastic first steps. It had been years since my rape, and I still refused to stay alone. Whenever Monty went out of town, I always stayed with friends. This was fine until Lauren was born. With a child, it became more difficult and burdensome. I knew it had to stop, but my fear was too strong. Many times, I had tried to stay alone and then at the last minute had given in and called a friend.

After my divine appointment with Pastor Craig, I made the decision to attempt one night alone. I was terrified. I prayed. Most important, I put into practice what I had learned in Philippians. I found my favorite verse on fear: "For God did not give a spirit of timidity, but a spirit of power, of love and of self-discipline" (2 Timothy 1:7). I placed this verse above my kitchen sink, on the mirror in my bathroom, and on my computer at work. I immersed myself in Truth. Finally the night arrived: Monty left for Austin. I turned on every television and every light in the house. I checked and double-checked every closet and every door. I set the alarm, shut and locked the bedroom door, crawled under the covers, opened my Bible, and held it close to my heart. Although I did not sleep much and heard every noise, I did it! I stayed alone! It was my first step to getting off my mat.

My night alone was a major victory! I gained a new confidence. However, my confidence was not in myself. It was Christ's confidence. I knew I would have some hard nights ahead as I persevered in this newfound determination to stay alone, but I was ready. Before my meeting that day, I believed I had every right to stay on that mat because I was the victim of an unspeakable crime.

My friend, you may feel the same way. You may justify staying on your mat because you have been wronged or are the victim of unfortunate circumstances. Maybe it is an abusive parent, a controlling spouse, a chronic sickness, the death of a loved one, or an addiction. The list of excuses is endless. But the choice is yours. Like the invalid in God's story, you can choose to remain paralyzed. Or you can respond to the call of Christ, get up off your mat, and walk. I encourage you to say, *Yes, Lord, I want to get well,* and allow Him to take your fears and anxieties and replace them with His peace . . . the peace that passes all understanding. He is waiting, ready to hold your hand and walk with you. Trust Him to take that first step.

CHAPTER SIX

Learning FORGIVENESS

Bear with each other and forgive whatever griev-ances you may have against one another. Forgive as the Lord forgave you.

—COLOSSIANS 3:13

LET ME TAKE YOU BACK to the days following my at-tack. One day as I left for work, I noticed a man walking through the parking lot of my apartment complex. As I watched him, I felt chills going up my spine. His height, his weight, and his gait seemed so familiar, yet I could not place him. Then he turned to-ward me; I saw his eyes, eyes I knew I would never forget. Shak-ing, barely able to speak, I ran to my apartment and called the police. They connected me with the detective on my case. I quickly explained what I had seen and demanded he come immediately and arrest this man. The officer calmly explained to me that they could not arrest him, but promised they would bring him in for questioning. Later that afternoon, they did bring him in but did not have enough evidence to hold him on the rape charge.

Days later, I learned that the police had questioned this man for Peeping Tom incidents around Baylor campus. Several coeds had reported seeing him standing naked in his apartment with the blinds open, exposing himself. In fact, one young coed identified him as the man who broke into her apartment in the middle of the night. Despite all of this new information, the police still refused to arrest him. They were of the opinion that Peeping Toms rarely progress to the crime of rape. I was so angry I was almost to the point of becoming irrational.

I became obsessed with punishing this man. I believed he raped me, and I wanted him to pay. Since we were unable to proceed with a criminal prosecution, I pursued a different route. I contacted the university and asked for a hearing to determine whether he was a danger to the campus. Along with my testimony, several of the young women who were witnesses of the Peeping Tom incidents testified against him. The university concluded that he was a danger to the campus and expelled him. He never received his degree. I hoped that would satisfy me. But it did not. As time passed, I continued to monitor his whereabouts. I wanted to know where he lived and what he was doing. I could not forget. I hated him and blamed him for everything wrong in my life.

For the months following my rape, my grandmother regularly called to check on me. During one of our conversations, she bluntly asked me if I had forgiven the man who raped me. Her question took me aback. I asked her how she, of all people, could ask me, the innocent victim, to extend forgiveness. He committed a heinous crime that I should never have to forgive. She cautioned that I would never recover from my rape if I continued to harbor a lack of forgiveness in my heart. I wanted to slam the phone down. It was only out of respect that I did not. Her words made no sense. *Why should I forgive him? He is the sinner. He is the wicked, evil one.* I was not ready to hear or receive her words.

My debate with God lasted for years.

In our next few conversations, she did not mention forgiveness. Instead, she shared verses from God's Word about trials. She explained that God uses them to grow us in our faith and make us more like Him. I politely listened. I wanted to understand. I wanted to find purpose in my circumstances, but I could not. She was asking the impossible. I could not imagine words of forgiveness ever coming from my lips. However, my grandmother was a godly woman. She loved the Lord, and she loved me. I trusted her and believed she had God-given wisdom from which I could benefit. I promised her I would think about the words she shared with me and would read my Bible to see what God had to say. I was scared because I knew somewhere deep within me that my grandmother was right.

God took me back to the Gospels. Each one vividly portrays the tremendous humiliation and physical suffering Jesus endured at the hands of His enemies. He received thirty-nine lashes (a scourging) at the hands of Roman soldiers. Following the scourging, the soldiers stripped Him and draped Him in a scarlet robe. They twisted together a crown of thorns and pushed it into Jesus' head. Mocking him every step of the way, the soldiers placed a staff in His hand and knelt before Him, calling "Hail, King of the Jews." Surrounding Him, they spit on Him and repeatedly struck Him with a staff. When Jesus was so weak He could barely stand, the soldiers ordered the Savior of the world to carry His own cross as they led Him to certain death. Upon reaching Calvary, the soldiers forced Jesus down on the cross and, stretching out His arms on the beam, drove nails into His hands and feet. His blood poured out.

It was as if I were reading these words for the first time. The reality hit me that Jesus did this for me. A deep sense of sadness and gratitude washed over me. Jesus, who "never sinned, never told a lie" (1 Peter 2:22 TLB), suffered physical and emotional torment for my sins that was beyond my human comprehension. Moreover, as Isaiah the prophet explained, "Yet it was the Lord's will to crush him" (Isaiah 53:10a). God planned for Jesus to suffer and die on that cross before the creation of the world. God poured out His wrath for me on His own Son.

When His tortured body and His crushed spirit could stand it no more, Jesus cried out, "Eloi, Eloi, lama sabachthani?" which is translated, "My God, my God, why have you forsaken me?" (Mark 15:34). What a beautiful act of submission to the will of His Father. In Hebrews it says, Christ "learned obedience" through suffering (Hebrews 5:8). Jesus submitted, knowing His obedience meant death and separation from His Father for the first time in history.

Jesus' next words penetrated my heart. Jesus prayed from the cross, "Father, forgive them, for they do not know what they are doing" (Luke 23:34). Jesus asked His Father to forgive the very men who had mocked Him, tortured Him, and finally murdered Him. Isaiah 53:7 tells us of Jesus, "He was oppressed and afflicted, yet he did not open his mouth; he was led like a lamb to the slaughter, and as a sheep before her shearers is silent, so he did not open his mouth." Jesus spoke not a word to His accusers and His torturers. When He finally did speak, His only words were words of forgiveness.

The question before me was this: If Jesus died to forgive my sins—if He asked His Father to forgive the men who nailed Him to the cross—what right did I have to withhold forgiveness from anyone, including the man who raped me? I debated with God. Jesus is Jesus. He is holy. He is perfect. He is God. I am not. I just could not believe God would expect me to forgive the evil this man had perpetrated against me. My circumstance was different. This man raped me. Rape is a vile, selfish act, worse than sins like gossiping, lying, stealing, or cheating.

My debate with God lasted for years. During this time, I heard a simple but profound story that went to the very heart of my question. It was yet another example of God speaking directly to me at the very time I was searching for answers. During a visit with prisoners on death row, Anne Graham Lotz, daughter of Billy Graham, met a woman who expressed uncertainty that Jesus' death on the cross was sufficient to forgive sins as grave as hers. Mrs. Lotz asked the condemned woman if she had ever been to the ocean and seen tiny holes in the sand where crabs darted in and out. The woman nodded yes. Mrs. Lotz then inquired if she had seen bigger holes where children had dug in the sand to make sand castles. The woman nodded yes. Then Mrs. Lotz asked if she had seen huge holes created by machines dredging for a channel or a ditch. The woman again acknowledged a quiet yes, looking baffled by her questions. Mrs. Lotz then asked what happens to all the holes when the tide rolls in: the tiny holes, the medium holes, and the big holes? A smile appeared on her pupil's face. Mrs. Lotz confirmed what the woman's smile revealed: the water covers the holes equally.

Mrs. Lotz explained to the woman that the blood of Jesus is like the tide; it washes over our sins and covers them equally. No sin is greater than another. God forgives them all through the shed blood of His Son, Jesus. Acts 10:43 says, "Everyone who believes in him receives forgiveness of sins through his name." There is further reassurance in Psalm 103:12: "As far as the east is from the west, so far has he removed our transgressions from us." This was a new concept to me. I grew up believing that some sins are worse than others. What Mrs. Lotz's story taught me is the beauty of God's grace. Grace gives what a person does not deserve.

I knew if I did not halt this train of thought, I would totally lose it.

I knew what I had to do. However, every time I sat down to pray, no words would come. I felt sick when I thought of forgiving my attacker . . . if I forgave him, he would be getting away with what he had done to me. I wanted him to suffer and hurt the way I did. *Surely, there is another way, Lord?* This man raped me. He is evil. He destroyed everything good in my life to satisfy his sick needs. I knew it was wrong, but to be completely honest, it felt good, it felt right to hate him.

In one of my darkest days during this battle with God, I read these verses in Psalm 139: "Search me, O God, and know my heart;

test me and know my anxious thoughts. See if there is any offensive way in me, and lead me in the way everlasting" (vv. 23–24). In this passage, David asks God to examine his heart and show him where he was not walking in step with God. I knew I was not walking in alignment with God's will, but I could not forgive. I confessed to God that I was not ready to do what He was asking.

During this tumultuous time, I learned that I was pregnant with Lauren. A decade had passed since my rape. Fear continued to control my life. My job as a young attorney occasionally required travel. Overnight trips stressed me out. Being in a new city, not knowing my surroundings, and staying alone in a strange hotel room heightened my already fearful state. This vulnerability aggravated my intense hatred for my attacker and made it more difficult for me to consider forgiving him.

One trip took our team to New Orleans to argue before the Fifth Circuit Court of Appeals. It was a privilege and honor for us to appear before this court, but I could not enjoy the moment because of my fear. After dinner that night, I returned to my hotel room and, as usual, could not sleep. Thoughts flooded my mind. *What kind of mother will I be? How can I raise a child when I cannot even cope with my own life? Would I ever allow her to go on a date alone with a boy? Would I let her go to college?* My heart raced; my stomach felt sick. I knew that if I did not halt this train of thought, I would totally lose it.

I reached for my Bible. It accompanied me on every trip. I opened to the parable of the unforgiving debtor. God took me to forgiveness . . . again.

Peter approaches Jesus and asks Him how many times a person must forgive his brother, knowing religious custom required only three. Peter, wanting to impress Jesus, suggests seven times. Jesus replies, "I tell you, not seven times, but seventy-seven times " (Matthew 18:22). Jesus did not intend his answer to mean literally 490 times. Rather, He was telling Peter to forgive as many times as it takes. He then told Peter this story:

Therefore the Kingdom of Heaven can be compared to a king who decided to bring his accounts up to date with servants who had borrowed money from him. In the process, one of his debtors was brought in who owed him millions of dollars. He couldn't pay, so his master ordered that he be sold—along with his wife, his children, and everything he owned—to pay the debt.

But the man fell down before his master and begged him, "Please be patient with me, and I will pay it all."

Then his master was filled with pity for him, and he released him and forgave his debt.

But when the man left the king, he went to a fellow servant who owed him a few thousand dollars. He grabbed him by the throat and demanded instant payment.

His fellow servant fell down before him and begged for a little more time. "Be patient with me, and I will pay it," he pleaded.

But his creditor wouldn't wait. He had the man arrested and put in prison until the debt could be paid in full.

When some of the other servants saw this, they were very upset. They went to the king and told him everything that had happened. Then the king called in the man he had forgiven and said, "You evil servant! I forgave you that tremendous debt because you pleaded with me. Shouldn't you have mercy on your fellow servant, just as I had mercy on you?"

Then the angry king sent the man to prison to be tortured until he had paid his entire debt. That's what my heavenly Father will do to you if you refuse to forgive your brothers and sisters from your heart. (Matthew 18:23–35 NLT)

How did this story apply to me? The king represented God. I was the debtor. He forgave my $10 million debt and was asking me to forgive a $2,000 debt. What was the debt? My right for revenge. My right to exact punishment on my attacker. If I did not forgive this debt, I would live the rest of my life in a prison of my own making. The parable ends with powerful words: "This is how my heavenly Father will treat each of you unless you forgive your brother from your heart." I thought, *Wow, God, You really know how to make Your point.* His Word could not have been clearer. I had no way out here.

Forgiveness does not come naturally.

The study notes led me to more Scriptures. God definitely wanted to drive this Truth home. First, He took me to the Lord's Prayer, in which Jesus tells His disciples to forgive others just as God had forgiven them. We need to "Make allowance for each other's faults, and forgive anyone who offends you. *Remember, the Lord forgave you, so you must forgive others*" (Colossians 3:13 NLT). In Ephesians 4:32, God directs: "Be kind and compassionate to one another, forgiving each other, just as in Christ God forgave you."

I heard God. He was clear, but how could I make my heart feel forgiveness? God showed me that forgiveness was not about feeling. It was a deliberate choice I had to make; moreover, to make it, my heart had to change. Scripture teaches that forgiveness requires a humble heart. Pride, the right to be right, must be set aside. Christ Himself is the ultimate example: "Your attitude should be the kind that was shown us by Jesus Christ, who, though he was God, did not demand and cling to his rights as God, but laid aside his mighty power and glory, taking the disguise of a slave and becoming like men. And he humbled himself even further, going so far as actually to die a criminal's death on a cross" (Philippians 2:5–8 TLB). Again, "Take my yoke upon you and learn from me, for I am gentle and humble in heart, and you will find rest for your souls" (Matthew 11:29). Scripture invites us to be like Jesus: "Be humble and gentle. Be patient with each other, making allowance for each other's faults because of your love" (Ephesians 4:2 TLB).

Forgiveness does not come naturally. A story about my son Bo illustrates this. Bo loves to play basketball after school with a group of friends. He looks forward to it every day. We schedule doctor appointments, haircuts, and playdates at least thirty minutes after school lets out so that he does not miss this great male-bonding time. However, on a daily basis I also witness his bickering and arguing over who fouled whom, whose rules are wrong, and whose rules are right. Occasionally, I have to intervene.

One afternoon Bo was involved in one of these scuffles. I called him out of the game and encouraged him to offer the first apology. His big blue eyes pleaded with me not to have to be the first one to say, "I'm sorry." I told him it was up to him, but he knew the right thing to do. I watched as he begrudgingly walked over to his friend, now turned enemy. I heard him grumble, "Sorry!" No eye contact, no smile, not a semblance of repentance or remorse.

Bo's heart mirrored mine. I easily could have spoken the words. Anyone can say the words. But God wanted more. He was asking me to extend genuine forgiveness from my heart. He needed me to humble myself. Sadly, I could not bring myself to do it. Why was it so hard? I misunderstood the true essence of forgiveness. I thought by forgiving, God was asking me to act as if my rape never happened, to forget the hurt and pain my attacker had caused. I could not do it. If I did, I would have said the words with the same grumbling heart with which my son uttered his.

God in His faithfulness did not give up on me. Using powerful words from Beth Moore, He showed me that He was not asking me to forget. My hurt and pain were valid in His eyes. They were real. However, I had allowed them to take control of my life. They ruled my heart, and as long as they did, God could not. I read these words written by Beth Moore and finally understood what God was asking: Forgiving means "handing over to God the responsibility for justice."[1] What was it about her words that broke through the barrier of hatred and bitterness around my heart? Knowing that she wrote these words after forgiving the person who sexually molested her as a child captured my heart. I needed her story. She experienced the same violation I had. Consequently, I knew she understood my pain. Her heart hurt as mine did. Her pain deadened her as mine did. Yet she was able to forgive. If she could forgive her molester, surely I could forgive my attacker. She acknowledged that although the memories were still painful, they no longer had *power* over her. Lack of forgiveness held her captive. Forgiveness set her free.

If I refused to forgive, I would never receive the full and complete healing God had in store for me.

Before that day, I lived by the rule that you forgive when you receive an apology because then you feel justified in extending forgiveness. In my situation, I knew I would never receive an apology. I would never come face-to-face with the man I had to forgive. By deferring the justice to God, Beth Moore explained that an apology was no longer an issue. I could forgive, free of any contingencies. I could freely forgive, trusting God to avenge me in His time, in His way.

You must be thinking that surely I would have forgiven him by now. But I could not. I held out hope that he would be caught and punished. I remained focused on me and on everything he had stolen from me: my dignity, my security, my confidence, my trust, my joy, and my peace.

Nevertheless, God pursued me. Why? God knew Satan was waiting for the opportune time to take advantage of my refusal to forgive. He would capitalize on it. With Satan, what starts as a simple sin will multiply and magnify in its intensity until it infects every relationship in a person's life, like cancer that starts in one organ and then spreads to invade every other organ. God, my Protector and Defender, did not want that for me. He orchestrated circumstances in such a way that forced me to choose Him. The circumstances were devastating but necessary to reach into the very depths of my unforgiving heart.

Every time there was an opportunity to identify my rapist and bring him to justice, God closed the door. Within twenty-four hours of my attack, the police located the knife, gloves, and mask in a ditch near my apartment. However, it was another dead end when the CSIs recovered no fingerprints since the man had worn gloves. When the authorities brought in the man who lived in my apartment complex, the one I suspected, he denied everything, so they released him. Every open door closed.

Then when I learned that the police had lost the physical evidence from my case, I knew the last hope of arresting my rapist was gone. God had closed every door. I was at a crossroad. What was I to do? The choice seemed obvious. I questioned God. *How could You possibly let this happen? Do You even know what You are doing with my life? Do You have a plan?*

Can you see how God had been speaking all along? I had the words of my grandmother, the teachings of other godly women, and the words of Scripture speaking to me. Yet I chose not to listen. I thought I was listening, but it was not until God took away every hope I had outside of Him to prosecute my rapist that I finally heard and obeyed. I found this verse: "Do not seek revenge or bear a grudge against one of your people, but love your neighbor as yourself. I am the Lord" (Leviticus 19:18). Romans 12:19 says, "Do not take revenge, my friends, but leave room for God's wrath, for it is written: 'It is mine to avenge; I will repay,' says the Lord." Punishment belonged to God, not me.

Over a decade after my initial conversation with my grandmother, I finally surrendered.

Her words came back to me: If I refused to forgive, I would never receive the full and complete healing God had in store for me. I will never forget the day. I sat alone on the sofa in my living room, speaking to a man who was not there. I could not see, feel, or touch him, yet I forgave him. I had no idea the depth of seething hatred and bitterness that entangled my heart until I spoke the words. Cleansing tears flowed down my cheeks like a never-ending fountain. As I cried, my chest heaved up and down, almost to the point of my being unable to breathe. I forgave my attacker not only for everything he did to me, but also for everything he had stolen from me. In that moment, God lifted a huge weight from my shoulders. A precious peace fell upon me.

Forgiveness came more easily to me from that day forward. His Word forever etched itself in my heart. His Truth seared into my soul. You see, when God changes us, it is not for the moment. It is forever, a continuous giving of Himself, never to be taken away.

My friend, has this lesson brought a name to your mind? Is there someone you need to forgive? Remember what I said when we began this journey together? You did not pick up this book by accident. You chose it because God has a message for you. He wants to speak Truth into your life. Will you yield your heart to Him? Will you trust God, take that first step, and offer forgiveness?

CHAPTER SEVEN

Surrendering Your STRONGHOLDS

*For God has not given us a spirit of fear and timid-
ity, but of power, love, and self-discipline.*

—2 TIMOTHY 1:7 (NLT)

I HAD BEEN TAKING baby steps on my journey to healing.
Little by little, God had spoken powerful Truths into my life, but
I still lived with the practical realities of being afraid. There were
nights I chose to stay alone, and I was proud of that accomplish-
ment. Most of the time, I still called a friend. Because we had lived
in Dallas for over ten years, we had a close-knit circle of friends
who generously opened their homes to my children and me when
Monty traveled. My kids saw it as a slumber party and received
lots of love and attention. However, it was a source of constant
stress for me.

When we moved to Charlotte, North Carolina, in 1998, I left
behind friends who were familiar with my circumstances, friends I
trusted completely. Our move thrust me into unfamiliar surroundings. Being a stranger in a new city returned me to a place of extreme vulnerability. Knowing there was no one to call if I needed

anything exacerbated my fears. This created a strain on our family and in our marriage. For eleven years, Monty had loved me through all of my issues, fears, and emotions. Without the network of friends to support us, the burden fell entirely on him. When he traveled, I did not sleep. Lack of sleep led to exhaustion. Exhaustion led to moodiness. I soon began to resent my husband for bringing me to this city so far from home.

I did have one friend in Charlotte, my college roommate Karen, who knew about my past and my daily struggles. She understood my fears. There were several nights when she opened her home to Lauren, Bo, and me when Monty traveled, but she had a husband and three children of her own. I could not impose upon her family indefinitely. Something had to give.

About six months after we moved to Charlotte, Karen invited me to her Bible study. It was my first true Bible study. I had participated in small group studies before, but this was my first time studying a specific book of the Bible from beginning to end. It was also my first time sitting under a Bible teacher. The thought of joining this study intimidated me, but I agreed because I knew it would allow me more time with Karen.

Our teacher, Jan Harrison, possessed incredible Bible knowledge. I had never met anyone who loved and believed in the power of God's Word as much as she did. Her passion was infectious. I found myself writing fast and furiously to record every word she spoke. Week after week I would go home, study my notes, and look up every Scripture she referenced.

Eventually we delved into the topic of *strongholds*. I was not familiar with this word. Jan defined a stronghold as any deeply rooted sin in your life that prevents you from growing in your relationship with God. She listed specific strongholds like bitterness, anger, pride, addiction, pornography, and fear. *Fear?* When she said the word, a shiver ran down my spine. Fear. I was afraid. In fact, fear controlled my life. *Could this be my stronghold?* I went home that night and reread the lesson and my notes, absorbing every word. I could hardly wait until we met again. I had so many questions.

As part of this series of lessons, Jan spent time discussing Satan. I knew who he was; I had learned about him in Sunday school as a child. Jan taught powerful biblical Truths about Satan that I had never heard before. I am going to spend significant time sharing what I learned because it has had a profound influence on my faith.

Who is Satan? God originally named him Lucifer, the star of the morning. God created him and all angels to serve and glorify God. Scripture tells us that in his original created state, Lucifer was the most brilliant and beautiful of all God's created beings in heaven. Ezekiel 28:12–15, 17 (NLT) describes him: "You were the model of perfection, full of wisdom and exquisite in beauty. You were in Eden, the garden of God. Your clothing was adorned with every precious stone . . . all beautifully crafted for you and set in the finest gold. They were given to you on the day you were created. I ordained and anointed you as the mighty angelic guardian. You had access to the holy mountain of God. . . . You were blameless in all you did from the day you were created until the day evil was found in you. . . . Your heart was filled with pride because of all your beauty. Your wisdom was corrupted by your love of splendor."

Over time, Lucifer's heart filled with pride. He was no longer content to worship and glorify God. He plotted to usurp God's throne. Lucifer wanted what belonged to God alone . . . all power and all authority on heaven and on earth. He orchestrated a rebellion in heaven, and as many as one-third of God's angels joined Lucifer in this battle. Scripture tells us that in response to Lucifer's actions, God cast him and his rebel angels out of heaven. 2 Peter 2:4 (NLT) says, "For God did not spare even the angels who sinned. He threw them into hell, in gloomy pits of darkness, where they are being held until the day of judgment."

Lucifer became Satan, also known by many as the Devil. Satan and his cohorts are committed to the destruction of all that is God's and of all that is good. He lives to lead God's people astray, to hold them captive, and to keep them in places of pain and despair. He has many methods, but his modus operandi is deception, to discredit and contradict the Word of God. John 8:44 (NLT) says that Satan "was a murderer from the beginning. He has always hated the truth, because there is no truth in him. When he lies, it is consistent with his character; for he is a liar and the father of lies."

What was Eve's first mistake? She entered into a dialogue with Satan.

I was a little overwhelmed and frightened by what Jan was teaching. Moreover, I wondered what it had to do with me. As if she could read my mind, our next lesson focused on the story of Adam and Eve. Scripture says that God created one man and one woman. He placed them in the beautiful garden of Eden. God created them in His image, and He deeply loved them. As created, Adam and Eve were pure and morally innocent. They did not lack for anything physically, spiritually, or emotionally. They reigned over the garden with complete freedom and only one restriction: God commanded them not to eat from the Tree of the Knowledge of Good and Evil.

One day as Eve was standing near the forbidden tree, Satan appeared to her in the form of a serpent. He asked her, "Did God really say you must not eat the fruit from any of the trees in the garden?" (Genesis 3:1 NLT). Satan twisted God's words for his own purposes. He knew God had told them not to eat of only *one* tree in the garden, yet he asked Eve if God told her she could not eat from *any* tree in the garden. Eve answered, "Of course we may eat from the trees in the garden. . . . It's only the fruit from the tree in the middle of the garden that we are not allowed to eat. God said, 'You must not eat it or even touch it; if you do, you will die'" (Genesis 3:2 NLT). While completing my homework on this particular lesson, I did not even notice the difference in Eve's words from God's original commandment. However, Jan pointed out that God did not say that Eve could not *touch* the fruit, only that she could not *eat* the fruit.

What was Eve's first mistake? She engaged in a dialogue with Satan. His leading question opened the door that caused her to misinterpret God's words to her. You see, Eve heard God's words with her ears, but she did not receive them into her heart.

Listen to the crafty Serpent's reply: "You won't die! . . . God knows that your eyes will be opened as soon as you eat it, and you will be like God, knowing both good and evil" (Genesis 3:4–5 NLT). God explicitly warned Adam and Eve that if they ate from the tree, they would die. Satan contradicted God. He cleverly convinced Eve that she would not die.

Satan denied the very truth God had given Adam and Eve. He suggested that it would be good to eat the fruit because in eating it, Eve would become "like God." He tempted her with power, prestige, and position. He led her to believe that God was withholding something from her, something more desirable than what she already had. As a result, Eve began to trust her evaluation of right and wrong, rather than allowing God's words to define right and wrong.

Eve had a choice: Believe God's Word or Satan's word. The choice seems obvious; she had so much to lose. However, Eve chose to believe the lies of the Serpent. She not only ate the forbidden fruit but also offered it to her husband, who ate it as well. The moment Adam and Eve took the fruit and bit into it, they lost everything. They damaged God's provision, His protection, and their perfect union with Him.

As Jan continued to share Eve's story with our group, I struggled to understand how it related to my life. Finally, Jan got to the point of her lesson. She explained that Adam and Eve are not fictional characters. They were flesh and blood, and the consequences of their actions were real. When Eve chose to partake of the fruit, sin entered the world. Satan gained a foothold on earth, and he continues his assault to this day. He is relentless in his attacks on God's children, using shame, guilt, lack of forgiveness, and fear to separate them from their Creator.

My thoughts wandered from the lesson when I heard the word *fear* again. *Stronghold. Sin.* God was speaking directly to me. I had come to recognize His hand at work in my life by now. God had led me to this study to bring me face-to-face with my fear. However, I was frightened. I remembered how many years I struggled with a lack of forgiveness and how difficult those years were. With God's help I had won that battle; however, I did not believe that I had the strength to do it all over again in relation to fear.

As my mind returned to Bible study, Jan had begun teaching on *spiritual warfare.* She took us to Ephesians 6:12—"For we are not fighting against flesh-and-blood enemies, but against evil rulers and authorities of the unseen world, against mighty powers in this dark world, and against evil spirits in the heavenly places" (NLT). She explained that there is an invisible spiritual conflict waging around us, an eternal battle between the visible world and the invisible world. She defined it as the battle between the forces of good and evil, light and dark. Her teaching seemed like fantasy, better suited for the movies or my son's PlayStation games than Bible study. She relayed that every person on earth is engaged in this war, even me. I left my lesson that day overwhelmed and afraid. I did not know what do with all the questions and confusion swimming around in my brain.

As soon as I got home, I put Bo down for a nap and sat quietly with God. I wept and prayed and wept and prayed. I was so tired of being afraid. I had lived with my fear for over a decade! It controlled my life, and I knew it was keeping me from a deeper, richer walk with God. As I closed my prayer, instead of asking God to take away my fear as I had for the last ten years, I asked Him to help me overcome it. It was a very different prayer. Taking away my fear meant asking God to do the work for me, whereas overcoming my fear meant that I had some work to do as well. I knew that God was not going to *take* my fear from me. He was calling me to be an active participant in the work He was about to do in my life.

With renewed commitment, I sat at my dining room table to study. I opened my Bible, asking God for wisdom to understand what He would teach me regarding fear and spiritual warfare. He had never failed me when I prayed to hear His voice. Sometimes it was slow in coming or I was slow in receiving, but He was faithful. As I began my search, I landed on Jeremiah 29:13–14—"'You will seek me and find me when you seek me with all your heart. I will be found by you,' declares the Lord, 'and will bring you back from captivity.'" Matthew 7:7–8 says, "Ask and it will be given to you; seek and you will find; knock and the door will be opened to you. For everyone who asks receives; he who seeks finds; and to him who knocks, the door will be opened." God is so gracious! These verses assured me that He was with me, listening, and ready to go to work.

His Holy Spirit is the One who empowered me to take my greatest step forward.

I eagerly dug into His Word for the answers I longed to hear. God took me back to the passage I memorized the first night I stayed alone in Dallas: "For God has not given us a spirit of fear and timidity, but of power, love, and self-discipline" (2 Timothy 1:7 NLT). *The Amplified Bible* says God has given us a spirit of a "calm and a well-balanced mind." I love those words, *calm* and *well-balanced mind*. This time I approached the verse in an entirely different manner. I did not just "read and recite" the words. I broke it down, studying and meditating on each phrase. As I did, questions came to my mind. *Spirit of fear. What is that? From where does it come?*

I knew who the Holy Spirit was. As a child, I learned that the Holy Spirit is the third person of the Trinity. Later in my teen years, I learned that when a person gives her life to Christ, the Holy Spirit comes to live inside of her. Jesus told His disciples this very Truth the night before He was to die on the cross: "But I tell you the truth: It is for your good that I am going away. Unless I go away, the

Counselor will not come to you; but if I go, I will send him to you" (John 16:7). *Counselor* is another name for the Holy Spirit. Earlier in John, Jesus explained, "And I will ask the Father, and he will give you another Counselor to be with you forever—the Spirit of truth. The world cannot accept him, because it neither sees him nor knows him. But you know him, for he lives with you and will be in you. I will not leave you as orphans; I will come to you" (John 14:16–18). I believed this, but I longed to understand how it happens.

Scripture makes it very clear that the moment we confess our sin and accept Christ as our Savior, God seals our hearts with His Spirit. Paul writes, "And now you Gentiles have also heard the truth, the Good News that God saves you. And when you believed in Christ, he identified you as his own by giving you the Holy Spirit, whom he promised long ago. The Spirit is God's guarantee that he will give us the inheritance he promised and that he has purchased us to be his own people. He did this so we would praise and glorify him" (Ephesians 1:13–14 NLT). We belong to Him.

The passage brought to mind another symbol of belonging that is extremely important to me—my wedding ring. When I put that ring on my finger, it marked me forever as Monty's wife. According to God's Word, the two of us became one. He sealed our marriage with His Spirit and His love, and my ring is a symbol of that covenant between God and us . . . for eternity.

What I am about to share with you is one of the most important truths I will write about in this book. I pray that you will understand the immense significance of the gift of the Holy Spirit. As we move through this chapter, you will see that His Holy Spirit is the One who empowered me to take my greatest step forward.

My friend, you may be having the same thoughts I initially had. God's coming and living inside a person seems far-fetched. Yet the Bible is unequivocal. Scripture clearly teaches that the moment you receive Christ as your Savior, God seals you with His Spirit. You immediately receive the fullness of His Spirit: not just part of God, but all of Him. The power of God, the same power that hung the stars, lined the planets in perfect order, transformed a void in space into a beautiful garden, and raised Christ from the dead comes to dwell within you.

I know it may be hard to believe, but it is TRUTH! *All* of God is in *all* of you *all* of the time. The presence of the Holy Spirit makes you like a "well-watered garden, like a spring whose waters never fail" (Isaiah 58:11). No more striving. You work in the strength and power of the God of the universe. Through that power, Scripture promises that God is able to "do immeasurably more than all [you] ask or imagine, according to his power that is at work within us" (Ephesians 3:20). God will do even more for you than you would dare to ask for yourself. He desires to give beyond your greatest prayers, thoughts, or hopes! This power is absolutely necessary to resist the guiles of the Devil.

Scripture warns that we have a great Enemy in the person of Satan. He is not a myth or product of human imagination. As I shared earlier, he exists and he is the fiercest enemy of God's people. Peter compares Satan to a roaring lion, prowling in search of prey (1 Peter 5:8). He has purposed in his heart to steal, kill, and destroy all that is God's and all that is good on this earth.

My kids and I love to watch Animal Planet. One Saturday afternoon we watched a fascinating special on lions, and Peter's words came to my mind. The reporter spent weeks observing a pride of lions. He followed one particular lion as she hunted her prey. After roaming for a time, the lion came upon a herd of antelope. For hours she lay in wait, pacing back and forth, watching for the opportune time to attack. The lion patiently waited until one of the antelope wandered off alone. She continued to watch to be certain no others from the herd followed the stray. Suddenly the lion appeared in sight of the antelope. She circled her prey. I could see fear in the antelope's body. Just as the antelope took its first step to run, the lion lunged with full force and brought the desperate antelope crashing to the ground. The victim struggled and fought but eventually succumbed to the determined predator. What a picture of Satan! He too waits and watches. He knows where we lack strength and easily spots our vulnerabilities. There is no doubt that he will pounce in our moment of weakness.

Peter explains that it is only in God's strength that we can defeat Satan. How? First, Christ's death on the cross freed God's children from Satan's power: "For he has rescued us from the kingdom of darkness and transferred us into the Kingdom of his dear Son, who purchased our freedom and forgave our sins" (Colossians 1:13–14 NLT). Second, the power of Christ infinitely exceeds the power of the Devil: "But you belong to God, my dear children. You have already won a victory over those people, because the Spirit who lives in you is greater than the spirit who lives in the world" (1 John 4:4 NLT). Finally, Christ will ultimately vanquish Satan forever: "Then the devil, who had deceived them, was thrown into the fiery lake of burning sulfur, joining the beast and the false prophet. There they will be tormented day and night forever and ever" (Revelation 20:10 NLT). God has provided for us the means to effectively overcome our foe. We need only to accept it.

You may think that my learning about the Evil One was adding to my fear. But strangely enough, that was not the case. Instead, I felt empowered. I was beginning to believe that God's Word truly would help me overcome my fear. Why? Because I was beginning to understand Satan, sin, and, most of all, fear. Satan was the source of my fear. Fear was my stronghold. Scripture says that I do not need to be afraid of Satan or to be held captive by my stronghold.

God explains exactly how to defeat Satan: "Stay alert! Watch out for your great enemy, the devil" (1 Peter 5:8a NLT). These words from Peter had authority because he spoke from personal experience. Peter failed Jesus in the garden of Gethsemane. His Savior and Lord asked him and the other disciples to stay awake and pray, but they fell asleep, not once but three times. Worse for Peter is that after promising Jesus he was ready to die for Him, Peter denied three times that he even knew Christ.

After Jesus' arrest in the garden of Gethsemane, Peter and John followed behind Jesus as soldiers led Him to the temple compound for His first trial. John followed Jesus into the temple courtyard, but Peter stayed behind. As he waited outside, a young servant girl asked him if he was one of Jesus' disciples. Peter responded, "I am not" (John 18:17). Peter then made his way over to a fire to keep warm. While standing there amidst His Lord's enemies, another person asked him if he was one of Jesus' disciples. Again, Peter denied his association with the Lord. Then one of the high priest's servants, a relative of the man whose ear Peter had cut off in the garden of Gethsemane, challenged Peter, "Didn't I see you with him in the olive grove?" (John 18:26). Peter again vehemently denied knowing Christ.

As the words tumbled from his mouth, Peter heard the unmistakable sound of the rooster crowing in the distance. At the same moment, Jesus turned and looked straight at Peter (Luke 22:61), and Peter remembered the words Jesus had spoken to him: "Before the rooster crows, you will disown me three times!" (John 13:38b). Peter fled into the night, and Scripture says that he "wept bitterly" for denying his Lord and Savior.

You and I are no different than Peter. Satan engages us daily in a battle for our hearts. What I want you to know and to believe is that the outcome of the heavenly battle is not in question. God is sovereign, and His victory was purchased on the cross at Calvary. God has already won! God, through Christ's death on the cross, not only guarantees victory for my soul and yours, but also guarantees victory for us every day in our battles with Satan. God's power is "far above all rule and authority, power and dominion, and every title that can be given, not only in the present age but also in the one to come" (Ephesians 1:21). God is telling us that we need not fear anything in all creation . . . not even Satan himself. Listen and believe these words written by John: "The reason the Son of God appeared was to destroy the devil's work" (1 John 3:8b).

Scripture encourages us to stand strong in the Lord and in His mighty power. Against Satan, our human effort is completely inadequate. God's power is invincible. As the lion with its prey, Satan lurks around every corner, waiting for an opportune time to attack. He will watch for our place of greatest weakness. Once he finds it, he will engage in a full frontal assault.

I had a weapon, and I knew I had to wield it!

It all began to make sense. After years of prayer, months of Bible study and personal quiet time with God, I realized that Satan was at the root of my fear. I had allowed his spirit of fear to fall upon me, and it controlled every part of my being. Satan saw me as a victim and began working on me the moment my rapist walked out the door. At every opportunity, Satan fired. I turned off the television the moment an announcer warned of a rapist loose in our city or the night a CSI episode involved a serial rapist. These were not coincidences. Satan knew I was trying to free myself from the prison of fear in which he held me, and he did everything within his power to keep me there. When Monty traveled, sounds I had never heard before emanated from my house, or the alarm would go off in the middle of the night for some unknown reason. Satan took every opportunity to return me to a place of vulnerability and weakness. He knew fear paralyzed me and left me ineffective as a wife, as a mother, and as a friend. Even more significant and most pleasing to him, I was ineffective for God.

In the early years following my attack, I was unaware that fear was Satan's work or that I had weapons to fight him. As I studied God's Word, I learned that I had not only weapons but also an arsenal at my disposal. Scripture tells me my greatest weapon is the armor of God. In Ephesians 6, God calls us to put on His armor daily so that when Satan's evil forces strike, we will be able to stand against them. With God's armor, we are ready for the battle. "Stand firm then, with the belt of truth buckled around your waist, with the breastplate of righteousness in place, and with your feet fitted with the readiness that comes from the gospel of peace. In addition to all this, take up the shield of faith, with which you can extinguish all the flaming arrows of the evil one. Take the helmet of salvation and the sword of the Spirit, which is the word of God. And pray in the Spirit on all occasions with all kinds of prayers and requests" (Ephesians 6:14–18).

Where was my battle taking place? In my mind. A spirit of fear had taken over, and the only way I was going to win was to fight using God's armor. Specifically, I am going to focus on one particular weapon, the sword of the Spirit, which is the Word of God. To defeat Satan you MUST stand on the Truth of God's Word. By now, I had been studying God's Word for years. Much of what I had studied was used by God to do a tremendous work to this point. Yet, despite more than a decade of asking God to take away my fear, I was still afraid.

My battle with fear reached an unmatched intensity by the time we moved to Charlotte, and had taken a toll on my family. So now, hope welled up within my heart. I had a weapon, an offensive weapon, and I knew I had to wield it! Until then, I had been praying for God to take away my fear, but I had never taken His Word and used it offensively.

Satan had placed a spirit of fear on me. I had allowed it to infiltrate every part of my being. I fed it, nurtured it, and gave it a place of priority in my heart and mind. Please do not misunderstand. Hear me clearly. Satan cannot physically enter God's children. We are sealed by the Holy Spirit, protected and loved by an all-powerful, all-knowing, and ever-present God. Satan cannot *make* us do anything. What he can do, however, is take advantage of what we do not know and use it to deceive us. He puts thoughts in our mind that lead us to places of lies and deception.

I sharpened my sword as I searched God's Word for more verses on fear; four stood out to me. First, Isaiah 41:10—"So do not fear, for I am with you; do not be dismayed, for I am your God. I will strengthen you and help you; I will uphold you with my righteous right hand." Next, Psalm 34:4—"I sought the Lord, and he answered me; he delivered me from all my fears," and Psalm 23:4—"Even though I walk through the valley of the shadow of death, I will fear no evil, for you are with me; your rod and your staff, they comfort me."

Finally, these verses pierced deeply in my soul: "He will shield you with his wings! They will shelter you. His faithful promises are your armor. Now you *don't need to be afraid of the dark any more, nor fear the dangers of the day*; nor dread the plagues of darkness, nor disasters in the morning" (Psalm 91:4–6 TLB). This last verse spoke loudly, as if God were sitting next to me, speaking directly into my ear. I feared the dark. At night, nightmares flooded my mind one after another. I awakened terrified, fully expecting to see the masked man standing over me, his cruel blue eyes inches from my face. I feared the day. *Should I get in that elevator? Should I park in that parking lot? Can I trust that man standing on the other side of my front door? Can I let the cable man in?* I was fearful twenty-four hours a day.

I took these verses and began praying them back to God. You see, the power in prayer lies in praying God's Word back to Him. It is His Word, and He must honor it. Isaiah writes, "So is my word that goes out from my mouth: It will not return to me empty, but will accomplish what I desire and achieve the purpose for which I sent it" (Isaiah 55:11). God did not put a spirit of fear in me, nor did He desire it for me. I trusted that He was fully able to take it away.

I am about to share with you one of the greatest moments in my journey to wholeness and healing. God took me from victim to victor. For years, I had prayed daily—and sometimes hourly—for God to take my fear away. Since learning these verses and the power in praying them back to God, my prayers had changed. They came from deep within me . . . a place I had never accessed before. I prayed from a faith I had never known before. I did not just believe *in* God—I *believed* God. I trusted and believed He was more than able to do what I was asking of Him.

It was a typical Tuesday evening. Monty had left for a business trip as he had done many times before, and I began my usual routine. I put my children to bed. I searched in closets, under beds, and in empty rooms. I turned on all the lights inside and out, turned on the alarm, and then the televisions in every room. I called my girlfriend Meg, and asked her to pray. Finally, I forced myself to go to bed. As I lay there, I felt compelled to turn off the televisions. I fought the urge at first, because I knew it meant I would hear every house noise. In the end, I succumbed. With the televisions off, I lay there in silence, waiting . . . waiting . . . waiting for the fear to come as it had done for fifteen years. I continued waiting for that sense of dread and fear that always came with the night.

It never did. Instead, I felt an overwhelming sense of peace and security! A feeling so foreign that I could not even remember the last time I felt it. Incredible! In that moment, I had a vision, a clear picture in my mind, of a wall of angels surrounding my house. After more than a decade of living locked inside a prison of fear, in one single moment it was gone!

Remember, I had called Meg earlier that night. Although it was now late, I felt compelled to call her and share my miracle. When I finished recounting my story, there was complete silence on the other end of the line. No words whatsoever. I was stunned. Why was she not joining in my praise? Finally, she spoke, and her words brought me to my knees . . . literally. Meg said that after I had called earlier in the evening, she and her husband had immediately prayed for me. He specifically prayed for *a wall of angels to surround my home*. I was astonished! His prayer was my vision. God's work was clearly evident. He wanted me to *know* that He alone was the reason for my newfound freedom. He did not want rationalizations and logical explanations to prevail. He wanted all the glory. That very night the spiritual battle for my heart was won in heaven. God's power and love defeated the spirit of fear that had imprisoned me for so many years. I fell on my knees before God that night and wept, praising Him for His faithfulness.

Please hear this Truth, my friend: God and God alone accomplished this marvelous work in my life. God's faithfulness, His goodness, His Word, His Truth, and His power set me free! Nothing more. Nothing less.

God not only answered my prayer but also my husband's prayers. For years, Monty stood by me, praying for and with me. He turned down many trips that would have benefited his career. Over the phone, he patiently listened as I poured out my fears when I was alone in the middle of the night. Without complaint, he patiently endured my irrational emotions and bizarre actions. God had shown His love and presence to me continually through my husband's steadfast love.

This time was different. I had peace in my heart.

God did for me what I could not do for myself. I had tried counseling, medication, books, talk-show advice, and even prayer. You name it, I tried it. Yet it was not until I surrendered myself totally to God, and trusted and believed Him at His Word that He set me free.

Do not be deceived, my friend. Satan continued to prowl. Two years later, in early August, my kids and I were enjoying a leisurely summer day at home. At about 10:00 a.m., I decided to return some books to the library. The library was less than a five-minute drive from our house. I thought of leaving the kids but decided against it since my son had a friend visiting. We left the house, drove to the library, and dropped the books in the return slot outside the building. We arrived home about 10:20 a.m. As I opened the door from the garage, I glanced into the den and noticed a window missing. Someone had taken it out completely. We had recently had work done on the house, so I thought that perhaps one of the workers had come to replace the window. However, I did not see a truck anywhere. The kids came in, and we called Monty to see if the contractor had called him about the window. Immediately, he told me to leave the house and dial 9-1-1. Within minutes, the police arrived, told us to stay back, pulled their guns, and entered the house. Since we had been gone only fifteen minutes, they were concerned the intruders might still be in the house. After a thorough search, they confirmed that burglars had broken into our home.

I walked into my dining room. The thieves had ripped the doors off my beautiful antique china cabinet in the dining room, and my silver was gone. I climbed up the stairs to my bedroom and discovered that all my jewelry was gone . . . every last piece. The burglars had dumped my entire jewelry box upside down and left nothing. Police filled my home, as they had on that day years ago. A crime team came to dust for fingerprints. They interviewed me and gave me a crime report to complete. It was reminiscent of June 7, 1986, all over again.

However, this time it was different. I had peace in my heart. The experience did not take me back to that place of fear and anxiety that imprisoned me for years. Yes, I was angry. Yes, I was devastated that my jewelry was gone, particularly my grandmother's heirlooms. God, in His faithfulness, protected me from returning to my stronghold. I was not afraid. In fact, I remember in the moment praising Him for prompting me to take my children with me and not leaving them at home alone. They would have been upstairs in the playroom, and the thieves would have come in, not knowing there were children upstairs. Who knows what could have happened?

That is not to say I was unaffected. I had Monty put better locks on the windows; we had the alarm company come to determine why the alarm did not sound, and I now hide my jewelry. This event should have sent me into a downward spiral, but it did not. I tell you this part of my story because I want you to see that God is bigger than anything Satan throws at us. When God gives victory, it is complete. You need never worry about it again.

Fear was my stronghold, but there are so many others. No matter your stronghold, God is fully able to remove it. He does not want anything to hold you captive, my friend. You have the power through His Word and His Holy Spirit to defeat your stronghold. It takes faith, work, and total surrender.

Do you have a stronghold in your life? Do you live your days controlled by something other than God's Holy Spirit? Do you feel locked in a prison? Do you want to make decisions from a place other than fear, worry, or bitterness? I challenge you to ponder the following question: Do you believe God is who He says He is and will do what He says He will do? If you do, surrender your stronghold to God, harness the power available to you in His Word and through His Spirit, and watch your prison doors fling wide open.

CHAPTER EIGHT

Quiet TIME

Be still, and know that I am God.

—PSALM 46:10

GOD HAD BROUGHT ME a long way since June 1986. No more bitterness. No more fear. What I felt was akin to what an inmate must feel as he exits his cell for the last time, having fully served his sentence. No more walls. No more chains. Freedom to come and go as I please. I could leave my house with confidence and return home without checking in every closet and under every bed. When Monty traveled, I slept in perfect peace. I was finally free from all that had imprisoned me.

As I settled into my newfound freedom, I began to ask myself, *Where do I go from here?* I had spent most of the previous decade struggling with day-to-day living. Now that God had delivered me from captivity, I had the desire to get out and live! Yet I had no direction . . . no idea what to do with my new life. Since I did not want to practice law at this point, I decided to get into volunteer work. I went into overdrive. I volunteered at our local rape crisis center, continued in my Bible study, taught high school Sunday school, served on our church worship committee, hosted a Bible study for kids in my neighborhood, and served at my children's school. Meetings, planning sessions, appointments, phone calls, and car pools filled my days.

In the midst of my busyness, several women from my Bible study invited me to attend a Christian women's conference. I was hesitant because I had never participated in such an event. Then I thought, *Why not?* I accepted their invitation. As we entered the Charlotte Coliseum on the first day of the conference, I was shocked. Thousands of women of all ages filled the arena. All present were eagerly anticipating the arrival of our keynote speaker, Beth Moore. I could not wait to hear her in person because of the powerful effect her written words had had on me as I struggled with forgiving my attacker.

> *"Lord, make it my deepest desire to seek You daily."*

Beth Moore spoke God's Word with commanding authority. She had a passion that electrified every heart in the room. Her prayers . . . I had never heard anyone pray as she did. She dropped to her knees, bowed her head, and talked to God as if He were sitting next to her, holding her hand. Her love for Him overwhelmed me. It was incredible. *Could I ever love God that much? Would I ever know God that well?* Only God could take someone who survived such horrific abuse and years of shame and despair and set her apart for such a divine calling. *Would God do that for me? Could God use me in such an influential way?*

As Beth Moore ended her teaching that day, she gave each of us a personal prayer assignment. She challenged us to pray daily for God "to show us more of Him." Those were her exact words. She promised that if we prayed this prayer, God would be faithful to honor it. When we walked out of the coliseum that evening, I left inspired to take the next step in my walk with God. That night, just before I crawled into bed, I wrote my prayer: *Lord, make it my deepest desire to seek You daily, and may my seeking You grow stronger as You reveal Yourself to me.*

I prayed my new prayer each morning before I got out of bed. As time passed, I prayed it more frequently. Sometimes I altered my prayer, including requests for my husband or for my children. Soon, deep within my heart, I sensed a newness and freshness in how I prayed. Something was different, but I was not sure what. You see, up to this point in my life, I had prayed mostly for the healing of others or for big things from God. Now I was praying to talk to God, to spend time in His presence. It felt a bit strange but so comforting.

I continued attending Bible study, and near the end of my second year, several leaders approached me about joining their leadership team. Curious, I asked, "In what capacity?" Jan responded, "We would like you to lead prayer." When I heard the word *prayer*, I had to refrain from laughing. Leading prayer meant praying aloud. The very thought of praying out loud in front of people, especially these people whom I admired so much, terrified me. Out of courtesy, I asked for more details, never intending to accept their invitation. Jan said that they had prayed about this and believed God was calling me to leadership as the prayer leader. I left our meeting dumbfounded: *Why would they choose me?* Nevertheless, I knew that when these women said they prayed, they prayed. If God gave them my name, then I knew this invitation was from Him. Why He had chosen me is what I was having trouble understanding.

A few days later, I took a leap of faith and accepted their offer with much fear and trepidation. So began the next step of my journey.

God impressed upon me that if I were to serve in this capacity, I needed to gain a heart of wisdom and understanding about prayer. I sought out and read every resource I could find on the subject. I discovered a consistent theme woven throughout the pages of each book. The key to prayer was quiet time with God. *Quiet Time.* I knew this was Christian lingo for spending time alone with God. What I did not know was exactly what this required. As I had done so often in the past, I went to my Bible to see what it had to say on the subject. I hope you are seeing a pattern in my life. Every time I need an answer, I go to God's Word.

Scripture teaches that God not only desires for us to spend time with Him, but also longs to spend time with us. "Come near to God and he will come near to you" (James 4:8a). Also, "For the eyes of the Lord range throughout the earth to strengthen those whose hearts are fully committed to him" (2 Chronicles 16:9a). God says in Jeremiah 33:3, "Call to me and I will answer you and tell you great and unsearchable things you do not know." Deuteronomy 4:29 says, "But if . . . you seek the Lord your God, you will find him if you look for him with all your heart and with all your soul." It became startlingly clear that God—the Creator of the universe, the Maker of heaven and earth, the King of kings and the Lord of lords—wanted to spend time with me.

Before I studied further about prayer, I committed myself to a more disciplined quiet time. For me, this meant waking up early in the morning, 5:30 a.m., since my kids had to be at school by 7:30 a.m. Rising at this hour was not easy. There were many mornings when I wanted to crawl back under the warm, cozy covers and go back to sleep for another hour. To be honest, on many mornings I did stay in bed. But on my good days, I got up, opened my Bible, and read. I did not use any outside sources; I let God be my guide. What He did was astounding. As time passed, I began to wake up on my own at 5:15 a.m. It was as if I had an internal alarm clock. We have a large walk-in closet off our bedroom. I would go in, curl up in the corner with my Bible, a notebook, and my dog to keep me warm. On the days when one of my kids got up early, meaning I could not have my usual quiet time, God helped me carve out time later in the day. God faithfully showed me that He was present and active in what I was doing. Often the Scripture I studied that morning proved to be relevant later in the day. At other times, God used what I learned in my quiet time or answered the prayers I prayed in a clear and direct way. God confirmed repeatedly that He was present and listening. My friend Lisa described it as God building my "faith muscles."

Examples of God's faithfulness fill my journal; here are a few of my favorites. Monty and I traveled to Hawaii for our tenth anniversary in 1997. While there, he bought me a beautiful gold Hawaiian heirloom bracelet and had it engraved with our wedding date. As I was getting dressed one day, I went to put on my bracelet but could not find it. I had worn it to church the Sunday before. Over the next few days, we retraced our steps, checking pockets, purses, cars, laundry baskets, and anywhere else we could think to look. In my journal that night, I wrote this prayer, *Please, Lord, let all things hidden be revealed.* After exhausting our search, my beautiful gift seemed lost forever. I continued to pray. Weeks later, April 30, to be exact, during my quiet time God impressed on my heart to check Monty's suit coat pocket. I immediately walked to the closet and reached my hand into the pocket. I felt something hard and round.

> *The more I sought God, the more I experienced Him. The more I experienced Him, the more I trusted Him.*

Much to my amazement and delight, it was my bracelet! Monty had worn that suit several times over the last several months, and we had checked the pockets the week we searched for the bracelet. Some would say we did not look hard enough, and it was there all the time. But I believe God heard my prayers, honored my quiet time, and revealed its hiding place. Why? To grow my faith muscles. He was teaching me to pray, to pray with great faith and trust.

One of my favorite answers to prayer involved the purchase of a car. Just a few months after I found the bracelet, I was on a quest to get a new car. When we moved to Charlotte, I quit practicing law to be a stay-at-home mom. Consequently, we had a limited budget on which to live. With two very active children, I joined numerous car pools to relieve drive time and gas consumption. Our current car did not always fit the number of children I needed to cart around, so I sought to enter the gas-guzzling, extra-large SUV car market. I asked Monty what we could afford. He replied, "Since our current car is paid for, zero dollars per month would be about right." My husband is famous for his sarcasm, if you can't tell! I told Monty I had chosen the Ford Expedition. He gave me a sweet smile and then warned me not to get my hopes up. On July 16 I wrote a prayer in my journal, asking the Lord for that specific car: *Lord, please provide us with this car. I ask that You would provide it within our current budget.*

After I had searched for months, Monty told me that if I could find a car that cost zero up-front and less than a certain amount per month, we could get it. Being realistic, he suggested that I lower my expectations and find something smaller and less expensive. In the quietness of my heart, I trusted God and continued to pray. Three months later, October 9, I was watching television while getting ready for Bible study. An advertisement for a car dealership caught my ear; I heard the words *going-out-of-business sale.* The announcer advertised four Expeditions at a certain price. When he repeated the price, I could not believe my ears. The amount exactly matched the amount that Monty said we could spend. After Bible study, I drove directly to the dealership, test-drove the vehicle, and called Monty to inform him that I had found our car. He prepared me for hidden costs and fees that would take it out of our price range. There were none. We bought it a few days later. Monty later admitted that he had mentioned a very low price just to lower my expectations. Amazing, isn't it?

Can you see God at work? He knew He was calling me to lead prayer. He also knew I was not ready or confident, so He had to teach me in small doses. He began with Beth Moore's challenge to pray for more of God. As she promised, the more I sought God, the more I experienced Him. The more I experienced Him, the more I trusted Him. The summer before entering my third year of

Bible study, I found Psalm 46:10: "Be still, and know that I am God." This verse motivated my quiet time throughout that summer. It would have been easy to stop, to sleep late with the kids, and then jump into the day midmorning. Instead, I chose to continue to wake up early (well, a little later than 5:15 a.m.) and spend time with the Lord. This incredible summer with God prepared me for leading prayer in my Bible study the following year.

However, when the school year began, commitments appeared on the calendar, activities increased, and stress heightened. I found it harder and harder to get a good night's sleep, so in the morning I was too tired to get up early. Before I knew it, my daily quiet times with God slacked off. Distractions entered my day, keeping me from spending time with my precious Lord and Savior.

This experience reminds me of when I first began dating Monty—I wanted to spend every waking minute with him. When I could not be with him, I wanted to talk on the phone with him. Outside of classes, sleeping, and football practice, we spent every minute together. Our new relationship was intoxicating. We had so much to learn about each other. As time passed, however, things became comfortable and less exciting. We no longer craved that time together. Other interests crept into our lives that soon came ahead of spending time together.

Similarly, in my relationship with God I craved quiet time with Him in the beginning and could not wait to hear what He had to say to me. But as my daily commitments increased, my quiet time decreased. My heart and mind, once consumed with seeking more of God, became preoccupied with life's responsibilities. Satan was again at work, but this time he camouflaged his activity. Earlier in my journey, Satan worked in obvious ways using fear and lack of forgiveness. Now he was subtle. He turned my focus to other things like my children, household responsibilities, work, and church activities. Notice how clever Satan is. He distracted me with responsibilities, which in and of themselves are not bad things. But they clearly interfered with my relationship with God.

If you are a mom, I know this day sounds familiar: Wake the kids, grab a shower, make breakfast, keep the peace, drive car pool, exercise, run errands, attend meetings. School's out. Car pool again, haircuts, dental or doctor appointments, homework, ball practice and cheerleading practice at the same time (how I can be two places at once I have yet to figure out!), dinner, PTA meeting, lunches to pack, ironing to do, bath time, bedtime. Wake up and do it all over again! I'm exhausted just writing this. For those of you who work full- or part-time jobs, this intense schedule is magnified. In addition, some of you reading this may be single moms. I applaud you. I have no idea how you do it!

If you are like me, the frustration of this lifestyle builds each day as the schedule picks up and commitments grow. There are never enough hours in the day. However, Scripture says God has a plan for our lives: "In his heart a man plans his course, but the Lord determines his steps" (Proverbs 16:9). The key to escaping an insane schedule is to learn God's plan for our lives. How do we discover this plan? It requires a listening heart. God clearly defines our priorities in Matthew 6:33—"Seek the Kingdom of God above all else, and live righteously, and he will give you everything you need" (NLT). Notice it does not say that He will give us everything we *want* but everything we *need*. God should come first. But for most of us, and I am especially talking to myself here, instead of centering our lives on God and letting all other things take their rightful place underneath Him, we center our lives on our agendas and fit God in where we can. We frantically rush from one activity to another, trying our best to keep it all together. At night we fall into bed utterly exhausted. On a good day, maybe we lift a quick prayer to God before we fall asleep.

Hear my next sentence very clearly, friend. This is NOT the life God desires for you. Yet, sadly, it is how most of us live. It happens innocently. In my busyness, I found it hard to spend the quiet time with God that I once did . . . the quiet time in which I journaled my prayers and recorded the answers, in which God gave me a verse in the morning and allowed me to use it later that day to bless someone else. Instead, now I came to God with hurry and a sense of duty. Quickly read a verse and move on; I cannot be late.

One particular afternoon my frustration peaked. What started as a peaceful afternoon ended in complete chaos after my children returned from school. My two angelic children, my own flesh and blood, morphed into horrible creatures before my very eyes. Creature One put on his favorite show as his reward for finishing his homework early and getting "on blue" (the highest award for good behavior) at school that day. (This fact will become ironic.) Creature Two, my middle schooler, burst through the door, slammed down her backpack, snatched the remote from Creature One, and changed the channel. Creature One immediately jumped off the sofa and reached for the remote, fully intending to get back rightful ownership. He demanded, "Give it back. I was watching that!" I am observing from the kitchen, my temperature rising. Creature Two slapped his hand out of the way, and Creature One latched on to her arm, grabbing for the remote. Creature Two yelled, "Your shows are stupid!"

Creature One countered, "I was watching first."

The barrage continued: "You are such a dork!"

"I am not!"

"YES, you are!" Creature Two lifted herself off the sofa, looking as if she were about to kill Creature One. As she walked past him on her way to the kitchen, she flicked him on the head. Looking at me, she demanded, "What's for dinner?"

At the conclusion of my response, I heard Creature One whining from the other room, "Why do we have to have that? Can't we go out for dinner tonight?"

By now, I was fuming. I yelled at the top of my lungs, *"Shut up!"* In our house, these are rarely uttered words, so they immediately silenced the Creatures. I launched into a tirade about their incredible selfishness, explaining how they made my life miserable, and informing them that I did not want to see them for the rest of the night, maybe even the rest of my life. I then sent Creature One and Creature Two upstairs crying and whining, "You are the meanest mom ever!"

As I listened to the Creatures crying, I realized the harshness of my words and the anger with which I spoke them. Did I really tell my children that they made my life miserable and that I did not want to be around them ever again? Yes, I did. Mommy of the Year, I am not. Incredulous at how easily I lost control, I began to weep. *How could this have happened? How could I have let it get this far?* I knew exactly how. I was tired, exhausted, and running on empty. I had not sat with the Lord on a consistent basis for quite a while. I had not been filling my heart with the things of God. It was completely empty, so when I needed strength outside myself, it was not there.

God was teaching me that I needed to come to Him *before* I reached this place of frustration and exhaustion. I opened my Bible to Psalm 62:8 and read, "O my people, trust in him at all times. Pour out your heart to him, for God is our refuge" (NLT). I had been spending every day operating in reactionary mode. I reacted to circumstances around me based on my emotions, on how I felt in the moment. The minute someone set me off, I lost it. When we allow ourselves to live like this, we hurt those we love most. The time we spend with God is paramount in determining the level of peace and contentment in our hearts.

Jesus teaches us this Truth through the story of Mary and Martha. These two sisters were dear friends of Jesus. Scripture reveals that He loved them very much and often visited their home. On one of Jesus' visits, Mary immediately stopped what she had been doing to sit at His feet and absorb His teachings. Martha continued working. Martha probably had spent the day preparing for Jesus' visit and upon His arrival was doing last-minute preparations. I suspect that drawers were slamming and pots were banging as her frustration with Mary's lack of assistance grew. Martha was doing all the work while Mary was lounging with the guests.

Finally, when she could take it no more, Martha came to Jesus and demanded, "Lord, don't you care that my sister has left me to do the work by myself? Tell her to help me!" (Luke 10:40).

I so identify with Martha. I too have the gift of hospitality. I am the one in the room who jumps up and says, "I'll do it" whenever there is a need for a place to gather. Martha continually opened her home to Jesus and His friends. She prepared a wonderful meal, a banquet fit for a King. She wanted to make everything perfect. I do too. When we host an event, I am the one cleaning the toilets, mopping the floor, setting the table, arranging the flowers, ironing the tablecloth, and dusting the chandelier. My husband is nowhere in sight. To be fair, if I ask him, he will help. (But you know how that is. You should not have to ask; they should offer!)

When the time comes for our guests to arrive, Monty makes his grand entrance, fresh from the shower. You will find him front and center, entertaining everyone with his clever quips, giving his captive audience every bit of his attention. I am in the kitchen *still working*, preparing the appetizers, putting finishing touches on the meal, and watching the rolls so they will not burn. Anger boils up inside me as I watch him in the other room, enjoying our guests and ignoring me. With a cutting edge to my voice, I call, "Monty, could you come in here and help?" I can barely speak his name because I am so angry. I will refrain from sharing the exchange that takes place in our kitchen upon his arrival! I know all of you Marthas feel my pain.

> *When you have experienced true quiet time with God, you know the emptiness of not having it.*

Was that what was going on in Martha's heart? Luke does not tell us. She seemed confident that Jesus would take her side, so she probably felt many of my same emotions. Interestingly, Jesus does not take her side. His answer is definitive: "Martha, Martha. . . . You are worried and upset about many things, but only one thing

119

is needed. Mary has chosen what is better, and it will not be taken away from her" (Luke 10:41–42).

Hear Jesus' words clearly. He was not telling Martha to be like Mary. He loved them both and knew them intimately. Jesus sat by His Father's side when He created each of them. Rather, He told Martha that Mary *chose* the better thing. There is a choice, and the choice has consequences. What do you think my dinner guests treasure when they leave my home at the end of the evening . . . the gleam in my serving bowl or the fun they had sharing stories with my husband?

Sound familiar? As it was Martha's choice, so it is our choice whether Jesus will take priority above everything else in our lives. Mary chose to sit at the feet of her Lord, to listen to His voice, and to know more of His heart. She made herself available. Mary models for us the act of worshiping, of resting at the feet of Jesus. Oh, what a comfortable place it is. God calls each of us to Himself: "This is the resting place, let the weary rest" (Isaiah 28:12a). He knew what Martha needed, and He knows what we need.

When you have experienced true quiet time with God, you know the emptiness of not having it. Time alone with God fills a place in our hearts that nothing else can. Scripture depicts this beautifully: "O God, you are my God, earnestly I seek you; my soul thirsts for you, my body longs for you, in a dry and weary land where there is no water" (Psalm 63:1). And in Psalm 42:1–2, "As the deer pants for streams of water, so my soul pants for you, O God. My soul thirsts for God, for the living God. When can I go and meet with God?" When we have a busy day, we rationalize: *I don't have time to go to Bible study, to pray, or to have my quiet time.* In reality, it is on our busy days that we need God even more. Henri Nouwen writes, "The very best thing that we need to do is set apart a time and place to be with God and Him alone."[1] God will pursue us, but He will never force His way into our lives. We have to make time for Him. No matter how *good* the good things are that keep us from spending time with God, they are not good enough.

The longer we deny God His time, the further we move away from His heart and His presence. Eventually we will be running on empty.

So far in this chapter, I have shown you the blessings of spending time alone with God. Practically, what does this time look like? The beauty of a quiet time is that there is no one correct way to do it. Let me share some ways to help you in your personal quiet time. I want to warn you that in the beginning, it may not come easily. Do not be discouraged. Never give up. Be persistent. Plan your date with God, commit to it, and protect that time at all costs. It is tempting to reschedule or cancel quiet time until a more convenient time, but that time will never come.

When I committed to spending time alone with the Lord, one of my first questions was what time of day I should set aside. God does not directly address time and place in His Word; however, if you examine Scripture closely, early in the morning seems the ideal time. David in Psalm 5:3 reveals his time: "In the morning, O Lord, you hear my voice; in the morning I lay my requests before you and wait in expectation." In Psalm 143:8 it says, "Let the morning bring me word of your unfailing love, for I have put my trust in you. Show me the way I should go, for to you I lift up my soul." Jesus Himself sets the same example: "Very early in the morning, while it was still dark, Jesus got up, left the house and went off to a solitary place, where he prayed" (Mark 1:35). This does not mean you must schedule your time with God in the morning, but Scripture continually points to this time as our model. It gives God a place of priority in your day. You are acknowledging that He comes first. There will certainly be fewer interruptions first thing in the morning. More than that, though, it is a beautiful way to begin your day. It sets your heart on the things of God and centers you before the hectic pace begins. An attempt to have quiet time later in the day is often pushed aside by responsibilities that just cannot wait.

For some, a morning quiet time may not be possible because of a job, newborn babies, small children, or school schedules. If you cannot meet God in the morning, find a time in your day that works for you. Once you commit to that time, turn off the phone, turn off the computer, and do not answer your door. Refuse to let anything interrupt your appointment with God. What matters to God is that you choose to meet with Him and make it a priority.

Where should you meet with God? Choose a comfortable place and meet Him there daily. It can be a room, a closet, a porch, or a special chair. The thought of being in your comfortable place should bring joy to your heart. When you are there, encourage your family to honor your time and not disturb you. My experience is that they will respect that time. In fact, as they begin to see a change in you, I guarantee they will welcome your quiet time and encourage it. I meet with God in the big walk-in closet in our bedroom, and Monty sneaks downstairs early in the morning and sits in the big leather chair in the den for his quiet time.

I know the thought of tackling the Bible can be daunting. It was for me. Do not be intimidated; there are many ways to begin. You can choose a particular book of the Bible. If it is your first time reading the Bible, I recommend selecting one of the Gospels (Matthew, Mark, Luke, or John) or maybe the book of Psalms. Read a few verses, an entire passage, or a chapter. Christian bookstores sell devotional Bibles, women's Bibles, and one-year Bibles. As you grow in your quiet time, add variety. There are devotional books, topical Christian books, and individual Bible studies available at Christian bookstores as well as at online ministries. If you still use your childhood Bible, I suggest you buy a new one. Look for a more contemporary translation. Buy a study Bible that has notes and history to enrich your reading. The most important thing is to stick to reading regularly.

As you begin each date with God, invite Him to join you. Ask the Holy Spirit to help you understand what you are reading. Scripture tells us to pray, "Open my eyes that I may see wonderful things in your law" (Psalm 119:18). Have a pen and notebook available to make notes, jot down questions, and record your thoughts and prayers. I started with a simple spiral-bound notebook. Thanks to friends and family, I now have beautiful journals in which to record my thoughts.

First, read the passage several times. Take some time to reflect on the words and phrases in the text. Ask yourself specific questions about what you are reading. For example, ask what the verses say about God, people in the story, Jesus, and God's character. Then, determine what lesson or idea the passage is trying to convey. Finally, prayerfully seek God for His words to you personally. Leave a blank space in your journal so you can come back later and note how and when God used that Scripture in your life. The stories I shared about my bracelet and the new car come from my journals, so I was able to quote you my exact prayers and the exact dates of these events. If a person's name or an event comes to mind while you are in your quiet time, write it down and note the date.

Be sure to carve out some time to pray, even if it is just a few minutes. I share in the next chapter an in-depth discussion of how to pray. There are also numerous books on the market to help guide your prayer time. I love Stormie Omartian's books *The Power of a Praying Wife* and *The Power of a Praying Parent*. She provides specific Scriptures and writes them out in the form of prayers.

Praying is simply conversation with God. In reading Denise Jackson and Ellen Vaughn's book *It's All About Him: Finding the Love of My Life,* I found this wonderful description of her perspective on prayer: "I was beginning to realize that heartfelt prayers are incredibly powerful—not just in how they change other people or circumstances, but in how they change me. There was no secret formula needed, no 'thees' or 'thous' or stilted language. The Bible guided me about who God really is, and I realized I could talk to Him as if I were sharing with one of my closest friends, pouring out my heart."[2]

Above all else, I encourage you to use your quiet time to meditate on and memorize Scripture. When defining a virtuous woman, Proverbs 31:26 says, "She speaks with wisdom, and faithful instruction is on her tongue." Psalm 119:11 says, "I have hidden your word in my heart that I might not sin against you." To speak words of wisdom or share faithful instruction, you first must know the Word that gives wisdom and instruction. "The mouth of the righteous man utters wisdom, and his tongue speaks what is just" (Psalm 37:30), and "Your commands make me wiser than my enemies, for they are my constant guide" (Psalm 119:98 NLT). Only when you have hidden God's Word in your heart will you be able to speak with His wisdom.

Scripture memorization transformed motherhood for me. My mothering left much to be desired when my younger child, Lauren, was preschool age. Whenever she disobeyed or threw a tantrum, my "go-to" emotion was anger. I would yell and often scream at the top of my lungs in response to her behavior. These confrontations always ended with my putting her in her room, slamming her door shut, and muttering hateful comments like "What did I do to deserve a child like you?" or "I'm going back to work so I don't have to be at home with such an unappreciative and disrespectful child." It breaks my heart now to remember my cruel and hurtful words.

As she grew older, Lauren's temper mirrored mine. We had screaming matches that ended with her in her room and with my raging with more angry and hurtful words. Often I would grab her by the arm and push her into her room before slamming the door. It is difficult for me to share this side of myself, but this is who I was for years. I did not want to react this way, but I seemed unable to help myself. Romans 7:14–15 (NLT) reflects my heart at the time: "The trouble is with me. . . . I don't really understand myself, for I want to do what is right, but I don't do it. Instead, I do what I hate." I hated who I was when I lost control.

One morning during Bible study, our leader Jan shared with us that as a young mother she had been angry and quick-tempered. This shocked me. She was such a godly woman, so mature and perfect in every way. She continued to share specific stories that sounded similar to mine. She testified to the power of God's Word in changing her heart. God replaced her temper with a tender and loving heart, one under His control. She learned to discipline her children in love. As I listened, I longed for what she had but thought it was not possible. My temper was ingrained in me. It was all I knew. It was who I was.

Jan hosted a weekend retreat for our leadership team. During one of our sessions, the retreat leader sent us off for a significant period of quiet time. As I sat alone with my Bible, I searched God's Word for verses on anger, patience, love, and discipline. As He led me to verses, I wrote them down in the form of a prayer. I asked the Lord to speak these Truths to me as I mothered Lauren and Bo. I asked God to fill my heart with His love.

When I returned home from that mountaintop experience, it did not take long for my testing to come. We had an incident that sent me over the edge. I sent both children to their rooms after I had lost control of myself. I ran to my room and threw myself on my bed, believing with every fiber of my being that I was a failure as a mother. I pleaded with God to help me. I felt helpless and alone. I knew I had already destroyed Lauren, if not both children, for life.

With God's Word, you are armed and ready to fight any battle the Evil One initiates.

When I sought God with all my heart, He imparted an undeniable Truth to me. Reading a few verses and reciting a prayer was not going to fix my problem. My symptoms—lack of patience, a heightened temper, an angry heart—were the hunger pangs of a parched and undernourished heart. I would find nourishment in one place and one place alone ... the strength and power of God's Word. In my quiet times, I focused on and memorized Scripture teaching me how to control my temper, how to have self-control, and how to discipline in love. I spent time in His Word every day, etching it into my heart and mind. Change did not happen overnight. The battle was long and challenging, but through the power of God's Word and His Holy Spirit, God's Truth prevailed! One particular day, I claimed victory.

My church sought a personal testimony for the Mother's Day service. Our women's ministry leader asked me if I would share. In light of the struggle I had undergone, I felt unworthy to give such a testimony, but I said yes. While preparing for my brief talk, I asked Lauren if she had noticed any change in me as a mother since I began spending more time with God. Her words were simple yet powerful: "Mommy, you just don't yell anymore." God used the simple words of a child to show me what a profound transformation He had accomplished in my life.

One of my favorite verses in Scripture stresses the high priority God places on His Word in our lives. "These commandments that I give you today are to be upon your hearts. Impress them on your children. Talk about them when you sit at home and when you walk along the road, when you lie down and when you get up. Tie them as symbols on your hands and bind them on your foreheads. Write them on the doorframes of your houses and on your gates" (Deuteronomy 6:6–9). These verses express the passion of my heart. In Psalm 119, God tells us that His Word strengthens us, comforts us, gives understanding, is true, is trustworthy, and is eternal.

As we end this chapter, I want you to see ever so clearly how God will use your quiet time to fill you with the ammunition needed to fight the everyday battles. Without His Word and His power, you are weak and defenseless against the guiles of the Evil One. You will fight only in your own insufficient strength. It is futile. But with God's Word, you are armed and ready to fight any battle the Evil One initiates. The battles are all around you. They are different for each of us, but you can count on this: victory is certain in Christ Jesus.

I pray that the stories and Truths shared in this chapter have further convinced you that God's Word is not just another timeless storybook full of tales of adventure and excitement. It is a powerful story, a love letter waiting to speak directly to you. Open it, read it, allow it to move and shape who you are. Scripture says that when Moses came down from Mount Sinai after receiving the Ten Commandments, "He was not aware that his face was radiant because he had spoken with the Lord" (Exodus 34:29). Moses' face literally glowed after spending time with God. Others could clearly see the presence of God reflected in him.

That is what will happen with you, my friend. Spending time with God, reading and studying His story will change your life. Your face may not literally glow, but the time you spend with God will profoundly affect your life and influence the lives of all those around you. Your countenance will shine with the love and life of the One who calls Himself the Light of the World. The beauty of the Lord will fall upon you, His holiness will wash over you, His grace will fill you, and His light will shine through you.

CHAPTER NINE

PRAYER

Devote yourselves to prayer, being watchful and thankful.

—COLOSSIANS 4:2

HER NAME WAS KATHLEEN. I had never met her, but the moment I heard her story, I began to pray. The burden I felt was unlike any I had felt before. It had been two years since I accepted the invitation to serve as prayer leader for my Bible study. What God taught me about prayer during that time prepared me for a giftedness that has brought me joy beyond measure. It has given me the opportunity to pray for the needs and hurts of others after spending so many years attending to my own. In this chapter, I want to share some of the faith-building Truths I have learned about prayer.

Doctors diagnosed Kathleen with pancreatic cancer at the age of forty-six. She had two beautiful children and a loving husband. The sweet aroma of Christ permeated every part of her being. Kathleen never met a stranger and saw every open door as an opportunity to share Christ's love. Even as she lay dying in her bed, she continued to minister to those caring for her, even complete strangers.

Although the doctors had given Kathleen six to twelve weeks to live, she deteriorated quickly. A woman once known for her strength and zest for life weakened with each passing day. One evening a group of neighbors and friends gathered in her home and prayed fervently and confidently for her healing. We trusted God would heal Kathleen as He promised in His Word. When I left her house that night, I waited expectantly for news of her healing.

Not long after that beautiful night of prayer, I received a call. Kathleen had died, six short weeks after her diagnosis. My heart was heavy with sadness not only for her family but also for those of us who surrounded her in prayer that evening in her home. We worshiped God; we cried out to Him; we prayed to Him, and it appeared He ignored us! Why pray if God knew what He already had determined to do?

Days later, I sat before the Lord in my quiet time, struggling to pray. I wanted Him to explain Himself. *Why did she die? Why did He not answer our prayers?* In the quietness I heard, *My precious child, I heard your prayer, and I know your heart, but I am sovereign, and it was her time to die.* It was then I realized that I lacked a true understanding of prayer.

I journeyed back in time through my notes, journal entries, and books to gain further insight into prayer. The first thing I learned was that mankind has not always had the privilege of praying to God in Jesus' name.

Before Jesus, Jewish law allowed one priest each year, the high priest who served in the tabernacle, the privilege of coming into the presence of God on behalf of the people. God called Moses to build a tabernacle for His people. Moses built it according to God's exact specifications. Within the tabernacle, a heavy veil separated two rooms. The room behind the veil, called the Holy of Holies, is where the priests kept the ark of the covenant. Scripture tells us that God Himself resided with the ark inside this holy room

(Exodus 25). Only the high priest had authority to enter behind the veil into the presence of God. This happened once a year when the high priest offered a perfect lamb, a blood sacrifice, to cover his sins and the sins of the Israelite people. The penalty for anyone found unlawfully entering the Holy of Holies was instant death.

Then Jesus came. Because of God's grace and His great love for His people, He sent Jesus to be the ultimate sacrificial Lamb. The coming of Christ eliminated the need for the high priest's annual blood sacrifice. Jesus shed His blood once and for all so that all people could have the opportunity to enter into God's presence through prayer, anytime, anywhere. The tabernacle curtain that had separated the people from God was gone, literally ripped in two.

Hebrews 10:19–22 explains, "And so, dear brothers and sisters, we can boldly enter heaven's Most Holy Place because of the blood of Jesus. By his death, Jesus opened a new and life-giving way through the curtain into the Most Holy Place. And since we have a great High Priest who rules over God's house, let us go right into the presence of

> *God does not care how eloquent our words sound. He simply delights in the fact that we come to Him.*

God with sincere hearts fully trusting him. For our guilty consciences have been sprinkled with Christ's blood to make us clean, and our bodies have been washed with pure water" (NLT). Scripture also says that at the moment Jesus cried out from the cross and gave up His spirit, "the curtain of the temple was torn in two from top to bottom" (Matthew 27:51). God, through the death of His Son, opened the way for you and for me to enter into His presence and pray anytime, anywhere!

That, my friend, is a wonderful gift. Sylvia Gunter wrote a marvelous book titled *Prayer Portions*. She describes prayer as "radically and gloriously encountering God, knowing Him better and loving Him more."[1] I love the words she chose: a glorious encounter with

God. There is no formula. God has no agenda. He simply delights in being with us. Scripture reinforces this: "For the Lord your God is living among you. He is a mighty savior. He will take delight in you with gladness. With his love, he will calm all your fears. He will rejoice over you with joyful songs" (Zephaniah 3:17 NLT). Can you imagine a more wonderful picture?

My daughter Lauren is fourteen and extremely busy with school, cheerleading, and friends. When she accepts my invitation to dinner, a movie, or a trip to the mall, I delight in every moment because between both our schedules, mother-daughter outings are rare. It does not matter what we do as long as we are spending time together. When we come before our Father in prayer, He feels much the same way. He has no expectations. God does not care how eloquent our words sound. He simply delights in the fact that we come to Him. His delight is so great that He rejoices over us with songs of joy.

Despite all I had learned, when I first began praying with my leadership team I felt inadequate. Their prayers were eloquent and rich. Mine were awkward and simple. I felt intimidated because I could not pray with the same depth and passion these women did. Over time, God opened my ears to hear and my eyes to see that they were not praying to impress me or anyone else. They were simply pouring out their hearts in the same way I saw Beth Moore pour out her heart at that conference. These women's words were inspired by the deep love they had for God and His Word. How I longed to pray as they did.

I shared this desire with one of my leaders. Wisely, she suggested that I look not to them but to Jesus as my model for prayer. Jesus maintained a consistent, active prayer life during His time on this earth. He did not pray to be changed or made more holy, for He was perfect. He prayed to communicate with His Father. Seeking time alone with His Father was one of Jesus' regular practices. Luke records that "Jesus often withdrew to lonely places and prayed" (5:16).

Jesus knew we would struggle with the concept of prayer, so He gave His disciples (and us) a model for prayer, commonly known as the Lord's Prayer.

> *"Our Father in heaven,*
> *Hallowed be your name,*
> *Your kingdom come,*
> *Your will be done*
> *on earth as it is in heaven.*
> *Give us today our daily bread.*
> *Forgive us our debts,*
> *As we also have forgiven our debtors.*
> *And lead us not into temptation,*
> *But deliver us from the evil one."* (Matthew 6:9–13)

This is a recipe for prayer. I love to cook. When attempting a recipe for the first time, I follow it exactly and gather all the necessary ingredients. As I grow more comfortable with the dish, I may add more of this, less of that, or even add new ingredients to suit my taste.

So it was with the Lord's Prayer. When I first began to pray, I followed Jesus' recipe. "Our Father in heaven, Hallowed be your name." *Hallowed* derives from the Greek word *hagiazo*, which means "to make holy, to make a person or thing the opposite of common."[2] The Lord's Prayer taught me to begin my prayers with praise, praising God for His love, His grace, His mercy, His power, His presence, and His sovereignty. Often we forget how much we have to be thankful for in having a personal relationship with the Creator of the universe and the Savior of the world until we focus our hearts on praising Him.

"Thy kingdom come. Thy will be done" (v. 10 KJV). Jesus' words direct us to ask for God's will, not our own, to be done in our lives. This is the hardest part of prayer and the one I struggle most to understand. Jesus sets the example for us. When speaking to His disciples, Jesus continually told them that it was not His will but His Father's will that motivated all He did. Listen to Jesus' prayer in the garden of Gethsemane: "My Father! If it is possible, let this cup of suffering be taken away from me. *Yet I want your will to be done, not mine* (Matthew 26:39 NLT). Again in John 5:30, Jesus says, "I can do nothing on my own. I judge as God tells me. Therefore, my judgment is just, because *I carry out the will of the one who sent me, not my own will*" (NLT). Scripture is clear. We must surrender our agendas to God's agenda, even when we do not understand or even see it.

"Give us our daily bread." What does Jesus mean by daily bread? He is referring to our daily needs. Listen to this excerpt from a prayer in Proverbs 30:7–9—"Two things I ask of you, O Lord; do not refuse me before I die . . . give me neither poverty nor riches, but give me only my daily bread. Otherwise, I may have too much and disown you and say, 'Who is the Lord?' Or I may become poor and steal, and so dishonor the name of my God." God knows that when we seek after too much or have too many riches, we may become proud and forget that He is the giver of every good and perfect gift that we have. Moses warned the Israelites:

> *When you have eaten and are satisfied, praise the Lord your God for the good land he has given you. Be careful that you do not forget the Lord your God. . . . Otherwise, when you eat and are satisfied, when you build fine houses and settle down, and when your herds and flocks grow large and your silver and gold increase and all you have is multiplied, then your heart will become proud and you will forget the Lord your God. . . . You may say to yourself, "My power and the strength of my hands have produced this wealth for me." But remember the Lord your God, for it is he who gives you the ability to produce wealth.* (Deuteronomy 8:10–14, 17–18)

God cares about the everyday events in our lives and wants us to come to Him with all our needs. But we need to be sure that we are not coming to Him with our greediness.

"Forgive us our debts, as we also have forgiven our debtors." I dedicated chapter 6 to this portion of the Lord's Prayer, in which Jesus calls us to forgive others as freely as we have been forgiven. Scripture makes it clear that to receive forgiveness, we must forgive others. Mark 11:25 says, "But when you are praying, first forgive anyone you are holding a grudge against, so that your Father in heaven will forgive your sins, too" (NLT).

"Lead us not into temptation, but deliver us from the evil one." Finally, Jesus directs us to ask God for protection from temptation and for deliverance from the deception of Satan, the father of lies. I talked earlier about how Satan prowls around like a roaring lion, seeking to devour all that is God's and all that is good. Only in God's power can we successfully battle Satan and the temptations and deceptions he throws our way. Pray in Jesus' name for the strength to resist everything that exalts itself against the will and authority of God in your life.

The Lord's Prayer is as relevant for our lives today as it was when Jesus uttered the words to His disciples over two thousand years ago. I encourage you to learn this prayer and make it your own. Have a conversation with God just as you would your best friend. And remember, do not only talk to God but listen as well. Listening is the hardest part. It is hard to quiet our hearts before God, but Scripture commands us to "be still, and know" that He is God (Psalm 46:10).

The beauty of prayer is that there is not only one way to pray.

Scripture also says to "pray continually" (1 Thessalonians 5:17). Some translations use the words "without ceasing." *Continually* means never stopping. Does this mean we must pray twenty-four hours a day, seven days a week, fifty-two weeks a year? The answer is both yes and no. In his book *The Purpose Driven Life*, Rick Warren writes, "Everything you do can be 'spending time with God' if

He is invited to be a part of it and you stay aware of His presence."[3] God wants to hear from us throughout each day. Whatever we are doing or thinking, He seeks to be included. Whether we are working, shopping, driving, or cleaning, God desires communication with us. By using the words "without ceasing," God is not so much referring to the actual time we spend praying but to the attitude of our hearts.

Let me share a story that brought this concept to life for me. Brother Lawrence, a medieval monk who lived in the mid-1600s, served as a cook in a French monastery. He taught himself how to pray without ceasing and records his experience in his book *The Practice of the Presence of God*.[4] Brother Lawrence purposely set out to experience God in his daily tasks. He admits that his journey was difficult, but he persisted, persevering day after day. Eventually, praying became habit. Brother Lawrence writes, "The time of busyness does not differ with me from the time of prayer; and in the noise and clatter of my kitchen, while several persons are at the same time calling for different things, I possess God in as great tranquility as if I were on my knees."[5] Brother Lawrence discovered that the key to unceasing prayer is to form a deep friendship with God. Whatever you do during your day, begin it alongside God for His glory. Praise God and share your heart with Him as you go about your daily tasks.

His story impressed me. However, Brother Lawrence was a monk. He spent most of his days praying anyway. In my busy world, I could not see experiencing God's presence in the same way. I was lucky to grab fifteen minutes first thing in the morning. However, as I began giving priority to prayer, I realized it was not my fifteen minutes of alone time with God that was at issue here. It was every other hour and minute of my day. I learned that continual prayer was not only possible, it was doable. It was a discipline, a habit I could develop. The reason I struggled was that I had a limited knowledge of what constituted prayer.

The beauty of prayer is that there is not only one way to pray.

Prayer comes in many forms, and each one puts us in remembrance of God in a different way. I was familiar with the standard, ordinary prayers I learned as a child, prayers that I added to little by little as I grew older. My grown-up prayers consisted of thanking God for His blessings and asking Him to help those who were sick or in need. This is how most of us learn to pray. However, there are other forms of prayer, which I will explore in the following pages.

In our darkest moments, we often cry prayers of desperation as we walk through a difficult or painful situation. On the cross, Jesus cried out, "My God, my God, why have you forsaken me?" (Matthew 27:46). In the midst of persecution by his enemies, David prayed, "My God, my God, why have you forsaken me? Why are you so far from saving me, so far from the words of my groaning?" (Psalm 22:1). The psalmist's words reflected my prayers after my rape, questioning God's love and even His existence. In our despair, we turn to God because we have nowhere else to go. Even our favorite soap opera characters pray these prayers. I can remember Erica Kane from *All My Children* in the Pine Valley Hospital chapel making deals with God if He would heal whichever husband or child was dying at the moment.

There are also prayers of confession. After King David slept with Bathsheba and Nathan confronted him with his sin, David cried out to God, "Have mercy on me, O God, because of your unfailing love. Because of your great compassion, blot out the stain of my sins. Wash me clean from my guilt. Purify me from my sin" (Psalm 51:1–2 NLT). In confessing, we ask for God's mercy, grace, and forgiveness. Real confession springs from a repentant heart and is difficult because it requires that we confront our sin. God's Word promises that "if we confess our sins to him, he is faithful and just to forgive us our sins and to cleanse us from all wickedness" (1 John 1:9 NLT). When we confess our sins to God, He cleanses us from the eternal effects of that sin. A confession removes the barrier that has existed between God and His people since Eve took her first bite of the fruit. John Piper writes, "Confessing sins is part of 'walking in the light,' which is what we must do if the blood of Jesus is to go on cleansing us from our sins."[6] My experience has been that when I deal with my sin before God, He not only forgives me but also blesses my obedience.

I discovered a new prayer in Richard Foster's book *Prayer: Finding the Heart's True Home*. He refers to it as a Breath Prayer and defines it as "a . . . simple prayer of petition that can be spoken in one breath."[7] It is a short prayer, usually one sentence that you can repeat throughout your day. To find your breath prayer, identify an area in your life that is a temptation, need, struggle, or even praise. For example, I struggled with patience. I searched my concordance and found Scriptures on patience. I chose 1 Corinthians 13:4, "Love is patient," and made it my breath prayer.

I prayed it as often as possible. In the beginning, I needed a trigger to remind me. At the time, I was on maternity leave, working from home, so I copied my verse onto several note cards and posted them throughout the house. I placed one in the kitchen and one in the bathroom. Every time I stood at either sink, the cards reminded me to offer up my breath prayer. Over time, I no longer needed the reminders. Praying the verse became habit.

Choose your verse and make it your habit. If you battle fear, you can pray, "I will fear not, for You are with me." Do you have trouble trusting God in your current circumstance? Pray "I will trust in You, Lord, with all my heart." Are you lonely or struggling in a relationship? Pray "Thank You that You will never leave me or forsake me, Lord."

Begin your prayer time seeking God first, not asking for your need.

Pray your breath prayer often, and through this prayer God will hide His Word in your heart.

My favorite prayer and the one that brings me my deepest joy is Intercessory Prayer. We invite God to work in and through us to affect the lives of those around us. Standing in the gap for others through this kind of prayer truly is the greatest privilege we have as Christians. The Bible promises, "The prayer of a righteous man is powerful and effective" (James 5:16b). All God asks for is a willing heart; He does the rest.

The key to any prayer, especially intercessory prayer, is praying the Scriptures. Hebrews 4:12 says God's Word is "alive and powerful. It is sharper than the sharpest two-edged sword" (NLT). Praying God's Word makes our prayers powerful and effective. Why? Because we are laying God's promises before Him and appropriating them for those for whom we are praying. For example, when Satan tempted Jesus in the wilderness, he took Him to the peak of a very high mountain and showed Him all the kingdoms of the world and their glory. "'I will give it all to you,' he said, 'if You will kneel down and worship me'" (Matthew 4:9 NLT). Jesus replied, "Get out of here, Satan. . . . For the Scriptures say, 'You must worship the Lord your God and serve only him'" (v. 10). Jesus rebuked Satan by quoting Scripture. He knew that His Father's Word was the most powerful weapon He had, and He used it against every temptation Satan presented.

I encourage you to begin your prayer time seeking God first, not asking for your need. Praise is one of the most powerful parts of prayer. Praise God simply because He is God and watch Him release His power in and through your prayers. Then, open your Bible and search the Scriptures. As you gaze into His Word, you will hear His voice and find His perspective on what to pray and how to pray it. This is where listening is more important than talking. When you pinpoint the Scriptures that speak to your heart, pray them back to God. I know it sounds complicated, but it is very simple. Let's try it together.

Lamentations 2:19 says, "Rise during the night and cry out. Pour out your hearts like water to the Lord. Lift up your hands to him in prayer, pleading for your children" (NLT). As a mother, I feel no greater responsibility right now than to pray for my children. By covering them in prayer, I release them into God's hands. I learned to pray the Scriptures over my children from the leaders in my Bible study. So I have done it every day since, and I have shared it with almost every mom I know. This may seem like a daunting task, but start with baby steps. In the beginning, select a few verses or an entire passage. You can pray for your children's salvation, for a love of God's Word, for trust in God, for wisdom, for joy, for a humble heart, or for a deep and abiding personal relationship with God. Here are some examples of short prayers I have written for Lauren and Bo over the years.

Lord, please provide an opportunity for Bo to receive the gift of salvation by Your grace through faith in Jesus Christ. (John 3:16; 2 Corinthians 7:10)

Hide Your Word in Lauren's heart so her desire is to please and obey You in all she says and does. (Psalm 119:11)

Help Bo to trust in You with all his heart and lean not on his own understanding and to acknowledge You in all his ways. (Proverbs 3:5–6)

Give Lauren wisdom beyond her years, Father. Keep Lauren pure by leading her to live according to Your Word. (James 1:5; Psalm 119:9)

Father, penetrate Lauren's heart with Your love, help her to love who You have created her to be, and ensure that she knows how long and wide and high and deep is Your love. (Psalm 139; Ephesians 3:18)

Give Bo a thankful heart and a contented heart. (1 Thessalonians 5:18; Philippians 4:11)

Clothe Bo in humility and teach him to put others first. (Ephesians 4:2; Luke 18:14)

Remind Lauren when she feels that she cannot accomplish what is set before her that she can do all things through You who strengthen her. (Philippians 4:13)

Grow Lauren and Bo in wisdom, stature, and favor with You and with man. (Luke 2:52, Daniel 1)

Father, teach Lauren to say, This is the day the Lord has made, I will rejoice and be glad in it, *no matter what her day may hold.* (Psalm 118:24)

I included quite a few examples, but I wanted to give you an idea of the many ways you can pray for your children. I took a verse of Scripture and incorporated it in a sentence to create a prayer from my heart. Praying this way for your children will build your faith. Scripture says, "Faith comes from hearing, that is, hearing the Good News about Christ" (Romans 10:17 NLT). The good news about Christ is the Word of God. Pray boldly and confidently. You are praying the mind and will of God as revealed in His Word.

The following is a prayer I wrote for Monty. No one stands in as strong a position as I do as his wife to pray for him.

Lord, I pray that You would open Monty's mind to understand Your Word. I pray that he will not be conformed to this world but be transformed by the renewing of his mind in Your Word so that he may know Your good, acceptable, and perfect will (Romans 12:2). *Please grant Monty wisdom, causing him to know Your mind. Keep him from pride and worldly temptations* (Job 33:14–17). *Help Monty to trust You with all his heart, not depending on his own understanding but acknowledging You in all his ways so he knows what direction to take* (Proverbs 3:5–6). *Father, open doors for Monty to tell others about You. Let his conversation be gracious and wise, for then he will have the right answer, Your answer. Give him Your words (Colossians 4:3–6). Grant him patience and perseverance when things are difficult (Colossians 1). Bless the work of his hands. Give him favor in the eyes of those for whom and with whom he works (Luke 2:52). Give him a discerning heart to know Your will and purpose for his life. Remind him daily to be anxious for nothing and to bring everything before You in prayer (Philippians 4:6). Finally, Father, help us to live together in perfect unity and love only each other all the days of our lives.*

You can use these same Truths to pray for your personal needs. For example, if you struggle with worry and anxiety, look up the word *anxious* in your concordance and find verses that apply. Read them, write them down, memorize them, and pray them back to God. Philippians 4:6–7 says, "Don't worry about anything; instead, pray about everything. Tell God what you need, and thank him for all he has done. Then you will experience God's peace, which exceeds anything we can understand. His peace will guard your hearts and minds as you live in Christ Jesus" (NLT).

Your prayer could read like this:

Father, I have so much on my mind right now. I cannot even sleep at night, I feel so anxious. Your Word asks me to pray about everything, so right now, Father, I am coming to You with my worries, especially _____. Father, I thank You for Your faithfulness. I thank You that You are in control of all things. I want to experience Your peace. So right now I am giving all of my worries to You, Lord, and claiming Your promise that in doing this, Your peace, the peace that passes all understanding, will guard my heart and mind. I thank You that I will be filled with Your peace from the top of my head to the tips of my toes. I trust You in this.

One woman in the young women's Bible study in which I teach took this lesson to heart. Marti struggled for years with infertility.

It consumed her every thought. Finally, she made a conscious decision to go boldly before God's throne and ask Him for what she wanted. Marti wrote this moving prayer using Genesis 1.

Lord, before this earth was created, it was formless, empty, and dark. In the same way, the emptiness that is my longing for a child is deep and waits for You to fill it. I boldly ask You to send me a child. Just as when You said, "Let there be light," I ask that You say, "Let there be a child for me and my husband." Lord, You are the Creator, the One who said, "Let us make man in Our image." You blessed them and said, "Be fruitful and multiply; fill the earth and subdue it." Please bless me so that I am fruitful as well.

Lord, I fully trust Your power to grant my prayer; I realize the power to create is in no other hand than Yours. To make a life is a wondrous thing. I give over to You my desire for a child, and I trust in Your ability to transform my heart. I promise to give You all the glory as Your will is accomplished. I ask for this in Jesus' name. I am Your servant. Amen.

Marti now has a beautiful, healthy child. She asked for what she desired deeply above all else and acknowledged that God alone had the power to grant it. Yet in the end, she fully surrendered her desire to Him. She believed He was more than able to do what she was asking, and she trusted her heart to Him.

We pray God's Word back to Him because He must honor it! True to His character, God cannot go back on His Word. Think about these two questions from your child: "Mom, can I have a piece of candy?" or "Mom, remember yesterday you promised me a piece of candy. May I have it, please?" Which statement resonates more strongly in your heart . . . the one in which your child simply asks for candy, or the one in which your child reminds you of your promise? The latter, of course. Do you understand what I am saying here?

It is important to realize that God's honoring His Word does not always result in a yes to your prayer, but be assured that His answer will be in line with His Word and true to His character.

When you begin, praying may feel awkward and uncomfortable. I promise you, sweet friend, it will be worth your time and effort. Remember, God has a plan for you and your family, but so does Satan. I warned you earlier of Satan's plan to steal, kill, and destroy all that is God's and all that is good. This includes your marriage and your family. Satan is a usurper and a divider. He will use any means possible to accomplish his dirty deeds. Satan cannot and will not be successful when you stand against him in prayer.

Claim Calvary's victory. Jesus is the Name above all Names. All authority on heaven and on earth is in Him. This authority is behind you when you pray to the Father. Jesus says in Matthew, "For who is powerful enough to enter the house of a strong man like Satan and plunder his goods? Only someone even stronger—someone who could tie him up and then plunder his house" (12:29 NLT). God is that stronger someone.

The prayers above focused on praying for yourself and your family, but intercessory prayer includes praying for any and all people God lays on your heart. I want to share a time when I prayed for my dear friend Karen's daughter. When Frances was two years old, she began to gain weight and had trouble urinating. One evening, her symptoms progressed to the point that her family rushed her to the emergency room. Doctors diagnosed her with nephrotic syndrome. In simple terms, her kidneys were damaged and were leaking large amounts of protein, so her inability to urinate caused toxins to build, poisoning every part of her tiny body. Even when the doctors stabilized her, she was unable to flush her body of the toxins naturally. Her doctors feared she would not make it through the night. They ordered dialysis as a last resort.

To say Frances hated dialysis is an understatement. She screamed in pain throughout the entire process. It was unbearable for Karen as she watched her precious baby fight to pull out the very tubes that were keeping her alive. One evening as I was sitting with Karen, the nurse came to set up the machine. The moment Frances saw it, she lost complete control. We forcibly held her down. It was agonizing. I wept as my hands held her down, and she looked into my eyes, wailing and writhing in pain. This scene continued for several days. Late one afternoon, in a moment of complete exhaustion and desperation, Karen cried out to the Lord, "Please let her pee, Father!" Her "prayer for pee," as it is now known, became the cry of all of our hearts. We passed this simple prayer through all the prayer chains. Karen prayed that prayer all through the night, joined via Internet by friends and strangers in Charlotte and all across the country.

The next morning, we had a miracle . . . a wet diaper! Frances urinated on her own, no machines, no drugs. Seldom has something so common, so unpleasant, ever become such a blessing. That wet diaper became a testimony to God's faithfulness. It was the beginning of her road to recovery. What doctors earlier in the week claimed would be a medical impossibility had now become a medical reality. God honored the prayers of a faithful mother and faithful believers. Karen is a living testimony of faith: "Faith is being sure of what we hope for and certain of what we do not see" (Hebrews 11:1). The doctors cannot explain what happened that one incredible night. But we can!

Although God hears all prayers because He is omniscient, according to His Word, He honors the prayers of those who ask in faith and ask *in His name*. Monty and I attended the presidential inauguration for George W. Bush in January 2001, at which Franklin Graham gave the invocation. He led our nation in a beautiful prayer, praying for President and Mrs. Bush, Vice President and Mrs. Cheney, the new administration, and our nation. He ended his prayer in Jesus' name. For days following his prayer, the media and others criticized Mr. Graham for being exclusive. But Mr. Graham was not praying to win a popularity contest or to please the media or even the president himself. He was praying in obedience to the very God upon whom this nation was founded. He prayed in faith in the name of the One to whom He was praying.

Praying in Jesus' name is essential. Jesus said to His disciples just before He went to the cross, "I tell you the truth, my Father will give you whatever you *ask in my name*" (John 16:23b). When we pray in Jesus' name, we pray in full assurance of the work Christ accomplished in His life, death, and resurrection, and His rightful position at the right hand of the Father. It is from that honored seat that Jesus intercedes on our behalf. Philippians 2:9–11 says, "God exalted him to the highest place and gave him the name that is above every name, that at the name of Jesus every knee should bow, in heaven and on earth and under the earth, and every tongue confess that Jesus Christ is Lord, to the glory of God the Father." Jesus is in whose name we pray. The following words reflect Jesus' genuine desire to answer our prayers: "I will do whatever you ask in my name, so that the Son may bring glory to the Father. You may ask me for anything in my name, and I will do it" (John 14:13–14). God certainly does not need our prayers to accomplish His work. However, is it not marvelous that He chooses to work through the prayers of people like you and me?

In our waiting . . . that is where we find God.

As we close this chapter, I want you to know that God tells us first to pray, and second to pray about *everything*. Many people mistakenly believe that we should only pray for significant and important life issues such as suffering, illness, and disasters, and only pray for others and not ourselves. Yes, we should pray for these things, but God's Word tells us to pray about everything in our lives. Philippians 4:6 is clear: "Don't worry about anything; instead, pray about *everything*" (NLT). First Peter 5:7 says, "Give *all* your worries and cares to God, for he cares about you" (NLT). There is nothing too small for God. He cares about even the seemingly insignificant things in our lives.

My friend Kim grew up believing that she should only pray for the "big" things. However, as she grew in her knowledge of the Bible, her understanding of prayer changed. She shared this wonderful story with me. She works full-time, and her job requires much travel. But Kim hates to fly. On one particular occasion, as her plane taxied down the runway, dark, ominous clouds filled the sky. Not long after takeoff, the plane began to experience turbulence. Moments later, she heard the pilot's voice over the intercom. He calmly asked the passengers to buckle their seat belts, explaining they would be flying through some rough weather for a time.

Kim decided to step out in faith. She prayed and asked God to calm the winds and take them safely and smoothly to their destination. Within seconds, the turbulence ended. Kim knew in her heart that God was not only present but also listening, caring, and comforting her. He grew her faith in answering that small prayer. Through a parable, Jesus says, "Well done, good and faithful servant! You have been faithful with a few things; I will put you in charge of many things. Come and share your master's happiness" (Matthew 25:23). When we pray in faith for little things, God will entrust us with the bigger things to pray for as we grow in our faith.

What about Kathleen? How do I reconcile Mark 11:24— "Therefore I tell you, whatever you ask for in prayer, believe that you have received it, and it will be yours"—with Kathleen's death? Why did God not answer my prayers and the prayers of so many faithful believers? I cannot give you a definitive answer. Only in heaven will we finally understand such mysteries.

However, when I finally understood the purpose of prayer, the answers to my questions no longer seemed important. It became clear to me that we pray in the physical. We pray for healing, deliverance from suffering, or relief from a heavy burden, and we want it now. We pray for things that might not be in our best interest. We ask for things that we are not yet ready to handle. God answers prayer in the Spirit. His concern is for our eternal well-being. We know so little about God's ways and God's timing. What we do know is that He will work while we wait.

In our waiting . . . that is where we find God. When we keep our eyes focused on the result, we miss the deep and precious work God is doing in our lives during that wait time. Oswald Chambers writes, "The idea of prayer is not in order to get answers from God; prayer is perfect and complete oneness with God."[8] We are to trust in the wisdom of God and ask for the grace to live in the wait. Learning to wait on God teaches us that our peace, our joy, and our relationship with Him do not depend on getting what we want. In John 12:24, Jesus says, "Unless a kernel of wheat falls to the ground and dies, it remains only a single seed. But if it dies, it produces many seeds." Sometimes we must relinquish our will in order to join God in His. He uses the waiting to change our heart's desire to align with His heart's desire. Paul says, "My old self has been crucified with Christ. It is no longer I who live, but Christ lives in me. So I live in this earthly body by trusting in the Son of God, who loved me and gave himself for me" (Galatians 2:20 NLT). Little by little, God transforms our wills, our hearts, and our prayers to be more like His.

Abiding in CHRIST

I am the vine; you are the branches. If a man remains in me and I in him, he will bear much fruit; apart from me you can do nothing.

—JOHN 15:5

THROUGHOUT THE WRITING of this book, I have prayed that God would speak personally to you through His Word and that no matter where you are on your faith walk, God would meet you there. Together, we have studied many principles of Scripture. I have shared many stories that I hope have encouraged you and touched your heart. However, I am most excited for the wondrous Truths to be unveiled in this chapter.

Never before had I felt as close to God as I did during my years in Jan's Bible study. The Lord healed my pain. He taught me to understand His Word, to hear Him speak, and to pray. He also gave me a place to serve Him. I was comfortable. I felt safe in my Bible study amidst so many godly women. Yet I still did not sense that passion for which I yearned.

During the fourth year of our study, Jan hosted a leadership retreat at her home to pray and plan for the following year. I left for the retreat excited for the future of our ministry and curious as to my role. Jan had invited a guest speaker, Renee, to share her testimony. As this woman unfolded her story, my heart immediately connected with hers. She had worked with a Christian ministry for years and loved it. She said it was a perfect match for the gifts and talents God had given her. Then her story took a surprising turn. God revealed to Renee through His Word that she was to leave her job, her comfortable place, for a place unknown. When I heard this, my chest began to pound. Her words struck a chord in my heart that frightened me. I came very close to running out of the room. Sadness washed over me as I felt the Lord impress upon my heart that He was calling me to leave my comfortable place.

As I drove home, tears flowed down my cheeks. *Leave? I cannot leave Bible study. This is where I learn; this is where I receive encouragement; this is where I belong.* I did not want to leave my safe haven. Yet, I was hearing God loud and clear. *What would I do? Where would I go?* Like Renee, I too had nowhere to go. I was leaving a place that I loved in order to go into the unknown. What was God doing? I did not understand.

I continued to attend Bible study and hoped that I was wrong about the message I heard. Yet each week in small ways, He confirmed that it was time for me to leave. I shared my fears with Jackie. She was my first leader when I joined the Bible study. We had become very close and roomed together on our retreats. She had mentored me over the last three years. Jackie suggested that I fervently pray for the Lord to show me His will in all of this. *His will? How would God reveal His will for me? And would I even recognize His will if I saw it?*

At the end of the spring semester, I left with a heavy heart. I spent the entire month of May engrossed in my Bible, searching for "God's will" even though I had no idea what I was looking for. Finding the answers to my earlier questions seemed so easy compared to this. I had key words like *forgiveness, worry,* and *fear* to guide my search. With God's will, I was unsure where to begin.

I prayed for the Lord to guide me, and He led me to John 15. I encourage you to read the entire chapter. John 15 begins with Jesus teaching about Himself as the True Vine and His disciples as the branches. Scholars believe that this teaching took place as Jesus and His disciples walked through a vineyard on their way to the garden of Gethsemane.

Remember, God's Word promises that it is living and active, so as you read this passage, place yourself in this scene. Listen carefully to Jesus' words. Imagine He is speaking directly to you. In John 15 Jesus explains how to live in a meaningful relationship with Him. It is not about what you are doing or how many times a day you do it. It is about connecting with and passionately pursuing Him. Jesus does not just want a casual relationship with you. Look at the words Scripture uses to describe this incredible relationship, words like *longing, yearning, hungering,* and *thirsting.* One psalmist prays, "As the deer pants for streams of water, so my soul pants for you, O God" (Psalm 42:1). David prays, "The one thing I ask of the Lord—the thing I seek most—is to live in the house of the Lord all the days of my life, delighting in the Lord's perfections and meditating in his Temple" (Psalm 27:4 NLT). Another psalmist writes, "How lovely is your dwelling place, O Lord Almighty! My soul yearns, even faints, for the courts of the Lord; my heart and my flesh cry out for the living God" (Psalm 84:1–2). David and the psalmists wanted to experience the fullness of God's presence in their lives above all else.

When you invite Christ into your life, the Spirit of the living God comes to live inside of you!

What is the one thing you desire? Is it happiness? Success? Wisdom? Peace? Wealth? Health? Long life? For years, I desired physical and emotional healing. God graciously gave me both. As wonderful as those were, they were not enough. I wanted passion like the kind I saw in women like Jan Harrison and Beth Moore. I wanted Christ to invade every part of me. I wanted Him to be the desire of my heart.

"I am the vine," Jesus said to His disciples, "[and] you are the branches. If a man remains in me and I in him, he will bear much fruit; apart from me you can do nothing" (John 15:5). In this verse, Jesus uses an everyday analogy to describe the relationship He envisions with His disciples. In fact, Jesus often used what was common and ordinary to teach His Truths. Jesus' words imparted that they were not simply His followers. They were connected to Him literally, just as branches are connected to a vine. The King James translation of this same verse uses the word *abide* instead of *remain*. Branches abide in a vine simply by remaining attached to it. They have no life on their own. It is only when branches connect to the vine that the sap can flow. As the branches abide, nutrients from the sap continuously flow into the branches to keep them healthy, enabling them to bear fruit. Separation from the vine means certain death.

Your heart abides in Christ in much the same way. First, you must connect to the True Vine. Attaching to the Vine occurs when you surrender your life to Christ. When you confess your sin, ask for forgiveness, and invite Jesus to be your Lord and Savior, God grafts you into the True Vine, His Son Jesus Christ. In that moment, God creates an eternal connection between your heart and His. It is through this connection that you will receive His "sap." God invites your hungry and thirsty soul to come to Him and abide in Him. In abiding, you will find tenderness, love, peace, joy, rest, and ongoing communication. In Him, you will receive direction, instruction, warning, and most precious to me: a fresh filling of God whenever you need Him.

Abiding seemed easier for the disciples. They literally lived with Jesus. They traveled with Him, ate with Him, slept with Him, and served with Him. But how do you and I abide in Christ? As with the branches, the key to remaining in Christ is the "sap." The sap is the incredible gift He gives us in His Holy Spirit. First Corinthians 2:9–12 says, "'No eye has seen, no ear has heard, no mind has conceived what God has prepared for those who love him'—but God has revealed it to us by his Spirit. The Spirit searches all things, even the deep things of God. For who among men knows the thoughts of a man except the man's spirit within him? In the same way no one knows the thoughts of God except the Spirit of God. We have not received the spirit of the world but the Spirit who is from God, that we may understand what God has freely given us." Although we studied this earlier, it bears repeating. The Spirit of God indwells every person who receives Christ as her Lord and Savior. My friend, hear this and never ever forget it. When you invite Christ into your life, the Spirit of the living God comes to live inside of you!

Max Lucado tells a wonderful story about an elderly woman who had a small house on the seashore of Ireland at the turn of the century. Because she was a wealthy yet frugal woman, the townspeople were surprised when she decided to be among the first in the town to put electricity in her home. Several weeks after its installation, a meter reader appeared at her door. He asked her how her electricity was working. She assured him that it was working quite well. He then asked her to explain to him why, if her electricity was working, that her meter showed scarcely any usage. "Certainly," she answered. "Each evening when the sun sets, I turn on my lights just long enough to light my candles, and then I turn them off."[1]

She had tapped into the power but did not use it. Her house was connected but remained unaltered by the incredible power available to her. I realized that I had been making the same mistake with God. I had surrendered my life to Christ. I knew Jesus lived in my heart. I knew the Word of God. I prayed. My heart was connected, but it was not altered by His presence. Accessing the power available in God's Holy Spirit requires that we flip on the switch and tap into His power. Tapping into His power can only happen when we abide in Him.

In its original translation, the word *abide* is *meinate*, which means to remain or stay. The dictionary defines *abiding* as "remaining in a fixed state or continuing in one place for a significant amount of time."[2]

A. W. Tozer writes, "We have almost forgotten God is a person and, as such, can be cultivated as any person can. . . . Full knowledge of one personality by another cannot be achieved in one encounter. It is only after long and loving mental intercourse that the full possibilities of both can be explored."[3] Communion with God through the Holy Spirit is the highest and most intimate form of communication you can have. When you seek God with all your heart, He responds by filling every part of you: your heart, your mind, your spirit, and your soul. Through His Spirit, He moves you to discern, to pray, to cry, to worship, to love, to rest, to act, and to obey.

What does this have to do with God's will, you ask? Through His Spirit He gives you the capacity to appropriate His Truth and make it relevant to your everyday life. When you need deep insight from His Word, He provides. When you need an added measure of understanding, He provides. When you need direction, He provides. When you need hope, He provides. When you need answers, He provides. God gives His Spirit without measure. Ephesians 3:20 says, He "is able to do immeasurably more than all we ask or imagine, according to his power that is at work within us." The more you abide in Him, the more He continually pours Himself into you. As my story will reveal, it is through an abiding relationship with Him that you come to know God's will for your life.

Many Scriptures speak of people hungering and thirsting.

You do not learn to abide in a classroom setting. You experience abiding as you do it. I cannot think of a better way to explain abiding and how it relates to knowing God's will than to share with you a series of my journal entries. It was May of 2003. I had just resigned from Bible study and journaled this prayer:

Father, why have You asked me to leave Bible study? I loved it there. I miss it so much. I don't understand, and I am searching for what You want me to do. Make it clear. Give me a spirit of knowledge and revelation. Point me in Your Word to what You want me to learn, to change, to do, to whatever! I am hungry to know Your plans for me. I am ready to accept whatever You give me. Do You want me to minister to the women in my life the way I have been ministered to? I am willing. Use my pain to bring glory to You. Thank You for Your promise that You will guide me into all Truth. I trust You, and I will wait on You.

I spent the summer continuing my search for His will. Through the months, God brought wonderful Scriptures across my path. I recorded the following verses in my journal, not fully understanding their relevance but knowing they were part of God's answer to my prayer.

John 4:14: *"But whoever drinks the water I give him will never thirst. Indeed, the water I give him will become in him a spring of water welling up to eternal life."*

2 Corinthians 9:10–11: *Now he who supplies seed to the sower and bread for food will also supply and increase your store of seed and will enlarge the harvest of your righteousness. You will be made rich in every way so that you can be generous on every occasion, and through us your generosity will result in thanksgiving to God.*

Jeremiah 29:11–13: *"I know the plans I have for you. . . . plans to prosper you and not to harm you, plans to give you hope and a future. Then you will call upon me and come and pray to me, and I will listen to you. You will seek me and find me when you seek me with all your heart."*

Jeremiah 33:9: *"Then this city will bring me renown, joy, praise and honor before all nations on earth that hear of all the good things I do for it; and they will be in awe and will tremble at the abundant prosperity and peace I provide for it."*

Isaiah 55:1–3: *"Come, all you who are thirsty, come to the waters; and you who have no money, come buy, and eat! . . . Why spend money on what is not bread, and your labor on what does not satisfy? Listen, listen to me, and eat what is good, and your soul will delight in the richest of fare. Give ear and come to me; hear me, that your soul may live."*

Many of the Scriptures speak of people hungering and thirsting. They point to God's Word as the means to satisfying that hunger and thirst. Second Corinthians 9:10–11 specifically spoke to my heart. God promised that He would provide the seed (the tools) for the sower (me) and bread (His Word) for whatever He called me to do. He also promised to supply all that I needed and even more. Jeremiah 33 says that in following God's will, I would bring joy and renown to His name. He was showing me that it was not about me but about Him. Because of these passages, I felt a peace that the burden was on God to reveal His plan; my part was simply to wait. My heart poured out praise for His faithfulness in this journal entry:

> *Oh, Father, as I prayed for You to reveal Your will for my life, I asked specifically if You are calling me to teach the women You have placed in my life. You opened me to Isaiah 55. I hear that as a "Yes," but I am so frightened to teach, to be vulnerable. Yet at the same time, the thought of teaching Your Word sparks great joy and passion within me. Please guide and direct me this morning on where and what You would have me do. I have sought You daily and will continue to trust You. I just want to be in Your will doing Your work . . . not*

mine! Is this Scripture a commissioning for my life? If it is, Lord, please give me confirmations. For I am scared and intimidated to teach Your Word, for who am I? I am not a scholar. I have no training. I am merely a life that has been transformed by You. I have my testimony. I offer it back to You. Help me to know what to do.

During this same time, I was memorizing Scripture. In early September, the Scripture God gave me for the week was 1 Peter 5:2–4: "*Be shepherds of God's flock that is under your care,* serving as overseers—not because you must, but because you are willing, as God wants you to be; not greedy for money, but eager to serve; not lording it over those entrusted to you, but being examples to the flock. And when the Chief Shepherd appears, you will receive the crown of glory that will never fade away." The first few words of this passage leapt off the page and into my heart. This verse was the confirmation for which I prayed.

Let me take you back a few years to give context to my story. When we moved to Charlotte, Lauren was nearly five and ready to start school. We enrolled her in a small Christian school where she thrived for three years. As third grade approached, we prayerfully considered moving her into the public school that was a five-minute walk from our house. Many of the kids in our neighborhood attended that school, and most of my friends had their children enrolled there. Part of me was frightened to take her out of her sheltered private-school environment, but Lauren did not live near any of her schoolmates and playdates were such an effort. After much prayer, we made the decision to move her.

Our calling is simply God's invitation to use our gifts and talents to His glory.

I decided that if I were going to take this step, I would join a prayer group to ensure that I still had the Christian connection with school. Much to my dismay, there was not a Moms In Touch or any other kind of prayer group at the school. After talking to a few other mothers, we committed to start one. We formed our group about the same time I stepped up in the prayer leader role at my Bible study. Coincidence? I think not!

We started small but grew little by little over the next few years. I usually began our time together with a Scripture and a short message, and then we prayed as a group. Our prayers were simple, but we saw God at work. We had one mom who wanted to join us but said she was uncomfortable praying aloud and made me promise not to ask. It was not too long ago that I had felt the same way. I knew exactly where she was coming from! I promised. By the end of our first year together, God opened her heart to pray aloud. As she prayed, joy washed over me. I will never forget that moment as long as I live. We experienced God move in powerful ways as we prayed for families, children, and teachers. By the end of our second year together, a few of the women were ready for more and asked if I would start a Bible study. Just hearing the words terrified me. At the time, I avoided committing to anything.

I did not realize until I read 1 Peter 5:2 that these sweet women whom I had joined in prayer and grown to care deeply for were the "flock" under my care. I had a strong sense that God had entrusted them to me. It was clear now what God's will was for me. He had called me out of my safe, comfortable Bible study to lead this tiny flock in a new Bible study. On September 13 I wrote:

Today I praise You for speaking so clearly through 2 Corinthians 9:10, Isaiah 55, and now 1 Peter 5:2–4 about leading women to You. Now that I know Your will for me, Father, please direct my steps. Be in every detail: where, when, book selection, who should come, etc.

Do you see how I started out with no knowledge of how to find God's will? One godly woman's advice encouraged me go to God's Word and ask. That I did. In seeking God through prayer and Scripture, His will became clear. My friend, there is nothing complicated about it. God designed you with a purpose. He has a plan for your life. His Word says, "For we are God's workmanship, created in Christ Jesus to do good works, which God prepared in advance for us to do" (Ephesians 2:10). God told Jeremiah, "Before I formed you in the womb I knew you, before you were born I set you apart; I appointed you as a prophet to the nations" (Jeremiah 1:5). God told me in His Word that He had a purpose for me to fulfill in His kingdom. I chose to believe God. I asked Him to reveal it to me and make it clear. He did. I knew in my heart that He intentionally had planted me in Charlotte, North Carolina, in my neighborhood, on my street, and in my home for this moment in time. It was not an accident. God carefully planned every step.

The same is true for you. There are many gifted women in the world. But YOU are the only one with your heritage, your life history, your convictions, your passions, your skills, your suffering, your heart, your appearance, your touch, your voice, your style, and your sphere of influence. God uniquely designed you for what He has called you to do. He planned every day of your life to lead you to your calling. I am living proof of this. Please know that our loving God will not waste any part of your life story, even that which seems horrific and hopeless. He intends to use every gift, every talent, and every life experience, good and bad, for His purpose and His glory.

I always thought that a calling was for ministers and full-time church workers. Scripture has taught me that a calling is not limited to full-time church ministry. In fact, for most of us it is not. Our calling is simply God's invitation to use our gifts and talents to His glory. It is that simple. We try to make it complicated. However, sometimes a calling requires a lot from us.

What if it is difficult? What if it takes you out of your comfort zone? What if it requires more than you are willing to give? I promise you the blessings you will receive as you seek to follow God's will far outweigh any amount of discomfort you may experience along the way.

The path to God's will for your life is clear. First you must surrender your doubts, your questions, and your fears to Christ. When you make yourself vulnerable and open your heart for Him to work, you are well on your way. Why? Because a surrendered heart is moldable and pliable. Please know that this process takes time. Be patient with God. Rick Warren writes, "God is never in a hurry, but he is always on time."[4] I waited seventeen years. Philippians 1:6 promises: "Being confident of this, that he who began a good work in you will carry it on to completion until the day of Christ Jesus." It may not be today. It may not be tomorrow. Trust that God, in His perfect timing, will not rest until He has you in the center of His will.

Over the summer months as I studied, wrote, and prayed, my friend Lisa had been praying as well. We both sought God's direction on starting this Bible study. Lisa was such a blessing. She had worked in women's ministry for years at our church. Her knowledge and wisdom, not to mention her heart for women, was invaluable. She promised me that if we heard yes from the Lord, she would walk alongside me in this endeavor. It was another confirmation from the Lord. God knew my insecurities, and He provided in Lisa all that I lacked. I had the passion and the call to teach; she had the wisdom and experience. When we finally received God's word of affirmation, we invited the women whom God laid on our hearts. The response was amazing. Every woman accepted our invitation, and a few even brought friends along.

As the time grew closer to start our study, I heard the lies of the Evil One whispering, *Who are you to do this? No one is going to come. You have no training for this.* Fear engulfed me. I prayed fervently for confidence, to hear God's voice. On September 26 I wrote:

Father, You have been so evident and present in my life these past months and years. You have spoken to me through Your Word as if You were sitting right next to me. You have brought me to this place. I know now You have a plan. You are inviting me to share Your

*Truths with hungry and thirsty women. As I now prepare to lead
Your sheep, please prepare the hearts of those You are calling. Give
them a hunger in their hearts, an open schedule, and a desire for fellow-
ship. Give me a love for each and every one . . . no matter who You
bring. Give Lisa and me guidance and direction, specifically, a mission
and a curriculum. Give us Your vision. Give me depth of insight and
wisdom as I embark on teaching for the first time. I love You, Lord.
I am scared, but I trust You to provide all that we need.*

My prayers were simple. I talked to God as I would a friend.
That is all abiding is, nothing more. Simply spending time with
God. Be honest with your feelings, share your dreams, confess your
fears, and admit your insecurities.

In October 2003, we held our first Bible study. I barely slept the
night before. I woke up feeling as I had in my first trimester of
pregnancy, nauseated and exhausted. I wanted nothing more than
to crawl into my bed and pull the sheets
over my head. I was terrified. How would I
start? Would anyone show up? What if
they hated it? What if they never came
back? As I sent my children off to school
and my husband out the door, I seriously
considered calling every woman and telling
her I was sick. Then Lisa arrived. We
prayed. We read God's Word. We prayed

*There is nothing more
glorious than being in
the center of God's will.*

some more. By the time the doorbell rang and the first woman
walked through the door, a deep sense of peace had filled my heart.
Christ's confidence rested on both Lisa and me.

He gave us the words to speak. We shared from our hearts and
gave each woman a chance to share as well. Their words revealed
God had been busily at work in our midst. The women were honest and vulnerable. Some women shared that they did not attend
church regularly and a few did not even own a Bible, so they were
scared and intimidated as well. They came for many reasons. A few

came because they wanted to be better wives and mothers. Others desired to deepen their friendships and take them to a new level. Many sought a closer relationship with God. It was beautiful to see how God drew each one. In different ways, God had given each woman a longing for more of Him.

Later that week as I reflected on what God had done, I wrote:

Father, where do I possibly begin? In the last few months, You have birthed a Bible study and answered the prayers of over twenty women. Thank You for each woman you drew here on Friday. Please fill Lisa and me with Your love for each woman, especially those we do not know. Set aside all that we know about our friends and give us a fresh start. Prepare each woman's heart to receive Your Word, to hear You speak, to be transformed, and to feel Your presence. Fill this home with the fullness of Your Holy Spirit every week. Open the hurting places in their hearts and heal each one.

Amazing, isn't it? I started out asking what I thought was a complicated question: How can I discover God's will for my life? The answer was quite simple. I found God's will by abiding in Christ.

I want to take you back to John 15:5 for a moment. It says that if we remain in Christ and Christ remains in us, we will bear much fruit. Learning God's will for my life was a magnificent by-product of my abiding. John 15 promises so much more. Jesus promises fruit as the reward for abiding in Him, and not just a little fruit, or some fruit, but "much fruit."

What is *fruit?* When you invite Christ into your heart, Scripture promises that you receive the fruit of God's Spirit. Galatians 5:22–23 says that the fruit of His Spirit is love, joy, peace, patience, kindness, goodness, faithfulness, gentleness, and self-control. A fruitful life is one characterized by Christ's love and peace. Fruit emerges by no effort of your own. It grows as you abide in Him. It is a life filled with His joy. Oh, friend, that is what I experienced: such incredible purpose and joy in bringing others closer to the heart of God! I felt so full of His Spirit during that time; it was if I would explode. There is nothing more glorious than being in the center of God's will. That is what I want for you!

I invite you to begin abiding today! For the next thirty days, commit to spending a few minutes with God each day in His Word. Before you begin, pray and ask God to reveal Himself to you. God will faithfully show up. Live expectantly. Listen for Him to speak. Look for Him to be at work. Ask Him to make His work evident in your life. Your small act of obedience, your commitment to abide will have far-reaching effects that you cannot begin to fathom. Before I started this journey, I would not pray aloud, even in front of my family. In my early law career, my legal briefs often came back heavily critiqued by senior partners. Every time I had to step into court to speak, I was terrified. I had no confidence in my ability to speak or to write. So when I first began speaking and writing, it stemmed from a heart of obedience, not because I felt talented or gifted in those areas. The first teaching I wrote and presented was on abiding. I wondered how it could possibly influence anyone.

Add God and the Holy Spirit into the equation and look what God and God alone can do. Here is a letter from a woman in response to my lesson on abiding:

Wendy,
I just wanted to thank you so much for the time you took this
year to share your incredible journey with us and for your
session on abiding in Christ. It is amazing you have endured
unimaginable heartache and pain and yet found Jesus suffi-
cient to supply your needs and heal your pain. It is powerful
to hear someone's struggles turned into stepping-stones for
Jesus to reach the lives of others. It is so obvious that each one
of those stepping-stones came about because you abided in

Him in the midst of your struggles. And now you are leading others to the hope found only in Jesus Christ. Thank you for sharing so beautifully.

CHAPTER ELEVEN

A New SONG

*I waited patiently for the Lord; he turned to me and
heard my cry. He lifted me out of the slimy pit, out
of the mud and mire; he set my feet on a rock and
gave me a firm place to stand. He put a new song in
my mouth, a hymn of praise to our God. Many will
see and fear and put their trust in the Lord.*

—PSALM 40:1–3

JUNE 7. EVERY YEAR on the anniversary of my rape, despite
my healing and the wondrous work God had done in my life,
something deep within me triggered a sense of sorrow and grief.
My body and soul intuitively remembered the extreme violation
they endured on that day so many years ago.

I had just returned from working out at the Y and jumped into
the shower. After a long and relaxing shower, I opened the door
and stepped out. For some crazy reason, in that moment I suddenly
thought of the date. It was June 8. The anniversary of my rape had
passed. After twenty years of memorializing that day and setting it
aside as a day of mourning and sadness, it had not even crossed my
memory.

Joy filled my heart and praise erupted from my lips! God had
promised me that I was a new creation, and now I truly knew that

I was. The old had gone. The new had come. A mighty work of God, supernatural and glorious.

A few days later in my quiet time, God placed Psalm 40 in front of me. He impressed these words on my heart just before I read it: *This is your life, sweet child. This is why I allowed so many years of pain and suffering in your life.* I then read the first three verses of Psalm 40: "I waited patiently for the Lord; he turned to me and heard my cry. He lifted me out of the slimy pit, out of the mud and mire; he set my feet on a rock and gave me a firm place to stand. *He put a new song in my mouth, a hymn of praise to our God. Many will see and fear and put their trust in the Lord.*"

Every word of this passage reflected my journey. After my attack, I had fallen on my knees before God, begging for answers. I waited, although not always patiently, as He revealed His Truths to me, Truths that lifted me bit by bit out of the mud and mire. He set my feet upon a solid rock, His Word, and taught me to stand confidently on that Word for my every need. He put a new song in my mouth, one that sings His praise, His hope, His joy, and His love. Dr. Reynolds's words from nearly two decades earlier came back to me. He gave me Romans 8:38–39, his life verse. At the time, I had no idea what he meant. However, when I read Psalm 40, I knew exactly what he meant. I had found my life verses.

God opened the doors for me to share my testimony.

As I continued in verse 3, it said that through my new song, many would see, fear, and put their trust in God. To whom would I sing this new song? Who were the many? I had no idea, but God knew. I began to write, compiling journal entries and Scriptures collected through the years. Day after day God opened my heart and poured forth the pages of this book. Of course, when I first started writing, I did not know what I was creating. I simply journaled my life experiences over the last twenty years.

One day as Monty pored over the pages of my work, he said,

"Wendy, this could be a book." At first, I rejected the notion because I am not a writer. In fact, Monty is the writer in the family. He has been published. Authors, not stay-at-home moms, write books. However, as I thought about Monty's comment and the words written on each page, I realized they told a story of hope, a story that God could use to draw others to Him so that they too could enjoy the healing and freedom that I had found in Him. God granted me the privilege of living out 2 Corinthians 1:3–4, "Praise be to the God and Father of our Lord Jesus Christ, the Father of compassion and the God of all comfort, who comforts us in all our troubles, so that we can comfort those in any trouble with the comfort we ourselves have received from God." Soon God opened doors for me to share my testimony. I took baby steps, speaking at small events and Bible studies.

In God's timing, I completed the book. However, I soon learned that writing a book and actually having it published are two different things. I tried on my own to contact publishers and sell my story, but with no success. I felt like the novelist John Grisham, whose first book was rejected by many publishers and agents, as letter after letter came back rejecting my manuscript. It was heartbreaking. Therefore, I resolved to stop pursuing publication and use the manuscript as material for teaching and speaking engagements.

Around the same time, a Bible study leader in Charlotte approached me about joining their teaching team. It was the perfect venue for me. The study attracted young women aged twenty-five to about thirty-five, many of whom were mothers. I loved teaching these women and sitting with them in small groups, hearing their hearts, and watching them experience God, many for the first time. The leadership invited me to their end-of-year celebration. I did not feel well that morning and had so much to do, but I went out of obligation. At the conclusion of the event, I met a woman named Bobbie Wolgemuth. She lived in Florida most of the year but owned a home in Charlotte to be near her two daughters. She "happened" to be in town visiting Lynn, the founder of our study. Bobbie and I immediately connected. She exudes the love of Christ. Her smile is infectious, and every word she utters is filled with encouragement. We spent the afternoon together sitting on her sofa, sharing our stories. It also "so happened" that her husband is a literary agent. He arrived at the house just moments before I left. We spoke briefly and then I went home. Little did I know what the Lord was about to do.

Bobbie contacted me the following week and asked me to send her sample chapters from my manuscript, which I eagerly did. After reading them, she begged her husband, Robert, to look at them even though he was not taking new clients. Soon afterward, Robert called and offered to represent me in my search to find a publisher for the manuscript. Isn't God amazing? When I gave up pursuing publication in my own strength, He stepped in and took over. He orchestrated circumstances so that not only did I find a publisher, but also I found a dear friend in Bobbie. Bobbie's wisdom and encouragement through the publication process have been invaluable, not to mention her faithful prayers lifted on my behalf. You are reading this book today because God ordained it to be. From June 7, 1986 to the day you purchase this book, God designed that our hearts, our stories would be intertwined.

Friend, I have loved sharing my story with you. We are approaching the last leg of our journey together, and I find myself sad that it must end. It is now time to go our separate ways. I wish I could sit with you and hear your story. Please know I am praying for you. I am trusting God to take His words and speak directly into your heart. I pray that in my story you have seen some of your own.

I want desperately for you to believe that God has a redemptive plan for your life and that no one and nothing can take that from you. No circumstance is too difficult, no choice too reprehensible, and no pain too deep for God to redeem. Before my rape occurred, God had set into motion His plan to heal and restore my broken heart. His only requirement was that I take the first step. I had to surrender my brokenness, my sorrow, my anger, and my pain and place it fully in His hands. When I took that step and sought Him for my answers, His redemptive plan immediately began to play out in my life.

Will you surrender your heart today? Will you take your first step? Will you place your sorrow, your brokenness, and your pain fully into God's loving hand? I promise you, He will transform your pain through the power of His Holy Spirit . . . the very power that raised Jesus from the dead. God will bring His comfort and mercy to the places where you have suffered pain and hurt. Whether your pain is from today, yesterday, ten years, or a lifetime ago, He is waiting to come in and heal you. Know that God will not force His way; He wants your permission.

Do not be afraid. Open all your hurting places, even the ugly and wounded parts of your heart. He knows them anyway. You may have tried to push past your painful memories or push them down deep into your heart and believe they are gone. But they will return. They will force their way back up and cause pain again and again and again. Believe me, I know.

Stand on the promises you have learned and humbly bow before your Father in heaven.

No drugs, no therapy, and no person, regardless of how well-trained or well-intentioned, can bring the full and complete healing that comes in the name of Jesus Christ. John Eldredge writes in his book *Waking the Dead:* "Christ is holding the broken parts of my heart in His hands, and bringing them all together, holding them tenderly until His life brought a wholeness or a oneness to what was many pieces."[1] God heals, mends, rebuilds, and restores.

As you take the steps in this book and surrender your hurting places to God, you will hear His voice speaking to you. Be persistent. Dig into His Word. Pray with all your heart. Stay in His presence. In addition, beware of Satan. Remember that he is the father of lies. He will come to discourage you, telling you that your situation is hopeless. He does not want your healing. Why? Because he knows that when it comes, you will be worthless to him. Redeemed lives full of the Holy Spirit, lives on fire for Christ, lives full of God's love are a terrible threat to Satan's kingdom. Consequently, he will try to paralyze and disable you during this time of healing. He will tell you that you are unworthy of God's time, that your situation is your fault, that you are hopeless, and that you are not strong enough. Do NOT listen to him. Let no condemnation, no lies, and no deception enter your thoughts.

You are exactly where God wants you to be. God will move the powers of heaven and hell to prevent Satan from drawing you back into your prison, your place of captivity. Stand firm on the promises of God. Stand in your rightful place as a child of God.

Sometimes the mountains along your journey will seem insurmountable. If that is the case, stand on the promises you have learned and humbly bow before your Father in heaven. Boldly ask God to move the mountain, believing in His promise that He is able to do immeasurably more than all you could ever ask or imagine through the power of His Holy Spirit. And sometimes He will move the mountain, but other times He may choose to leave it. You must then go before God, asking for wisdom on how to attack it and for strength to climb it, claiming His promise that you can do all things through Christ who strengthens you. Either way, God will manifest Himself mightily. During these times on your journey, He will reveal Himself in real and personal ways. Surrender it all to Him. Seek Him with all your heart. I promise you on the authority of God's written Word, He will not let you down.

My heart pounds as I write the last words of this final chapter. I want to be sure of one thing before I say farewell: that you have the opportunity to connect to the True Vine. In the last chapter, we talked about abiding and the necessity of connecting to the Vine before you can abide. Have you ever connected to the True Vine?

Have you ever surrendered your life to Christ? Do you have the assurance that if you die tomorrow, you will spend eternity with your heavenly Father in the home He has prepared especially for you? If you have never invited Christ into your life, I invite you to ask yourself these questions:

1. Do you know God as your Creator?
2. Do you know you are a sinner and that Jesus Christ, the Son of God, died on the cross for you and is the only acceptable sacrifice God will accept for your sin?
3. Do you know that as your Savior, Jesus has forgiven you all your sins and you are now a new creation, meaning that the old things in your life are gone and every part of you is new?
4. Do you know that the moment you accept Jesus' gift of salvation, Jesus sends a part of Himself to live within you in the person of the Holy Spirit?

If you are ready to answer yes to these questions, my heart is overjoyed! Friend, pray this simple prayer and enter into the most glorious relationship you will ever experience, an eternal, abiding relationship with your Savior and Lord, Jesus Christ:

Father, I know that I am a sinner, and I am sorry for my sin. I repent of my sin. I believe that Your Son, Jesus, died on the cross for me, and I receive Him now as my Savior. I give my whole life to You and want to make You Lord of my life from this day forward.

If you prayed this prayer, know it is the beginning of an amazing journey. Find a church or Bible study to help you grow in your newfound faith.

If you cannot answer yes to these questions, please know that God continues to walk alongside you, drawing you closer to His heart with every Scripture you read and every prayer you pray. Ask the Lord to show you what it is in your life that keeps you from believing and receiving His Son. As you pray, remember His promise that when you seek Him with all your heart, you will find Him. God will meet you right where you are.

Let me seal our time together in prayer:

Heavenly Father, I invite You into my life. Sometimes it is hard for me to understand why You have allowed pain and suffering, and at times I have been confused and angry with You. But now, at this moment, I am ready to surrender my hurting places to You.

Thank You for the words of Truth You have revealed to me. Take them now, plant them deep within my heart, let them take root and flourish within me. Bring Your transforming power into my life. Heal and restore me. From this day forward give me eyes and ears to see all that You desire to teach me. Help me to trust You in all things. I give You total access to my heart, the heart You created and specially formed for me. Bring the fullness of Your Spirit into my heart; shine the light of Your Word into my darkness. Come and meet me here.

I love You, Lord. I ask all this in the powerful name of Your Son, Jesus Christ my Lord. Amen.

NOTES

Chapter 2: Why Did God Allow This?

1. James Strong, *Strong's Expanded Exhaustive Concordance* (Nashville, TN: Thomas Nelson, 2001), Hebrew and Aramaic Dictionary, No. 2451, 87.

2. Ibid., 86.

3. Lawrence Richards, *It Couldn't Just Happen: Fascinating Facts about God's World* (Dallas, TX: Word, 1987), 12.

4. Paul Dowswell, *The First Encyclopedia of Space* (England, Usborne Publishing Ltd.).

5. Ibid.

6. Billy Graham, "Love Immeasurable," *Decision*, February 2002, 4.

Chapter 3: God's Story Unfolds

1. "Active." Dictionary.com. Random House, http://dictionary.reference.com/browse/active.

Chapter 4: Treasures in the Darkness

1. *Matthew Henry's Commentary on the Whole Bible: Complete and Unabridged* (Hendrickson, 1991), 2397.

2. Nancy McGuirk, *Rest Assured: Devotions for Souls in a Restless World* (Nashville, TN: B&H Publishing, 2007), 56.

3. James Strong, *Strong's Expanded Exhaustive Concordance of the Bible* (Nashville, TN: Thomas Nelson, 2001) Greek Dictionary, No. 571, 34.

4. Beth Moore, *Breaking Free: Making Liberty in Christ a Reality in Life* (Nashville, TN: Lifeway, 1999), 55.

5. Francois Fenelon, *Let Go* (New Kensington, PA: Whitaker House, 1973), 28.

Chapter 5: On the Mat

1. James Strong, *New Strong's Expanded Exhaustive Concordance* (Nashville, TN: Thomas Nelson, 2001). Greek Dictionary, No. 3309, 160.

2. Elisabeth Elliot, *Keep a Quiet Heart* (Ann Arbor, MI: Servant, 1995), 98.

Chapter 6: Learning Forgiveness

1. Beth Moore, *Breaking Free: Making Liberty in Christ a Reality in Life*, (Nashville, TN: Lifeway, 1999), 104.

Chapter 8: Quiet Time

1. Henri J. M. Nouwen, *The Way of the Heart: Desert Spirituality and Contemporary Ministry* (New York, NY: Harper Collins, 1981), 31.

2. Denise Jackson with Ellen Vaughn, *It's All About Him: Finding the Love of My Life* (Nashville, TN: Thomas Nelson, 2007), 148.

Chapter 9: Prayer

1. Sylvia Gunter, *Prayer Portions* (Birmingham, AL: The Father's Business, 1995), 10.

2. James Strong, *Strong's Expanded Exhaustive Concordance of the Bible* (Nashville, TN: Thomas Nelson, 2001), Greek Dictionary, No. 37, 2.

3. Rick Warren, *The Purpose Driven Life* (Grand Rapids, MI: Zondervan, 2002), 88.

4. Richard J. Foster and James Bryan Smith, eds., *Devotional Classics: Selected Readings for Individuals and Groups* (San Francisco, CA: Harper, 1993), 81.

5. Ibid, 82.

6. John Piper, *A Godward Life: Book Two* (Sisters, OR: Multnomah, 1999), 104.

7. Richard Foster, *Prayer: Finding the Heart's True Home* (San Francisco, CA: Harper, 1992), 122.

8. Oswald Chambers, *My Utmost For His Highest* (Uhrichsville, OH: Barbour, 1963), 160.

Chapter 10: Abiding in Christ

1. Max Lucado. *Just Like Jesus* (Nashville, TN: Word, 1998), 8.

2. "Abide." Dictionary.com. http://dictionary.reference.com/browse/abide.

3. A. W. Tozer, *The Pursuit of God* (Camp Hill, PA: Christian Publications, 1982), 13.

4. Rick Warren, *The Purpose Driven Life* (Grand Rapids, MI: Zondervan, 2002), 222.

Chapter 11: A New Song

1. John Eldredge, *Waking the Dead: The Glory of a Heart Fully Alive* (Nashville, TN: Thomas Nelson, 2003), 139.

Guide for
REFLECTION
AND STUDY

CHAPTER ONE
VALLEY OF WEEPING

1. Do you currently have a loss, a hurt, or trial that is burdening your heart?
   a. How does this burden currently affect your life?
   b. Have you tried to deal with this issue through means other than God?
      (1) If yes, what have you done?
      (2) Did it successfully resolve any of these issues?

2. How would you characterize your faith in God?
   a. I am not sure there is a God.
   b. There is probably a God, but I do not know Him.
   c. I have some faith and it's growing.
   d. I have a strong faith.

3. If you chose *c* or *d* above, has the hurt or pain that you shared in question 1 affected your faith? Has it made you question God's love, His goodness, or the Truth of the Bible? Explain.

4. Are there emotions flowing from this pain that strongly control your life (anger, jealousy, fear, resentment, etc.)? If there is more than one, prioritize them from strongest to weakest.

5. Do these emotions affect you daily? If yes, do they also affect those around you? Explain how.

6. If you have a hurt, a burden, or a struggle you are carrying right now, I invite you to open your heart, even if it is just a little bit, and allow God access as you begin your journey through this book. Even before this book was published, I prayed for every woman who would one day read it. I prayed specifically for you, my friend, that you would come to know God in a new and fresh way.

Now that you have this book in your hand, let me pray for our journey together:

Heavenly Father, we acknowledge You as our Creator and the One who loves us just as we are. Together, my new friend and I come before You and give the next weeks to You as we begin this journey together. Lord, I ask that You open her heart to receive all the wonderful Truths You have in store for her. You led her to choose this book because You have a powerful work You want to perform in her life. I pray that as she turns each page, she would experience the power of Your healing touch. Thank You for Your promise that when we seek You with all of our heart, we will find You. I claim that for her right now. I pray she will experience You in a powerful way. We thank You in advance for all You will do. It is in Your Son Jesus' name we pray. Amen.

CHAPTER TWO
WHY DID GOD ALLOW THIS?

1. List five characteristics of God that you knew before you opened this book.

2. In this chapter, you learned that God is sovereign. *Sovereign* is defined as possessing supreme power.

   a. Does knowing God is sovereign comfort you or make you more confused in your circumstances? Explain.
   b. What does 1 Timothy 6:15 tell you about God?
   c. What does Jeremiah 10:12 tell you about God?

3. You also learned that God is wise.

   a. Read Romans 11:33 and share what it tells you about God and wisdom.
   b. Read James 3:13–18 regarding wisdom.
      (1) Describe heavenly wisdom.
      (2) Describe earthly wisdom.
      (3) What is the difference?

4. God's wisdom extends not only to His creation (the earth and stars), but also to you personally. Read Psalm 139:1–18. What do these verses tell you about how God knows you?

5. Finally, you learned that God is love. Scripture tells us God loves unconditionally with an everlasting love.

   a. What does Romans 8:38–39 tell you about God's love?
   b. What does that mean to you personally?
   c. Can you feel that love and trust in your current situation? If not, explain why not.

d. Do you remember a time when you really felt God's love? What were the circumstances?

e. Was there a time when you felt abandoned by God? What were the circumstances?

6. Ponder the following words describing God. Has God ever been any of these to you? Which ones and why?

a. Deliverer

b. Counselor

c. Bread of Life

d. Strong Tower

e. Redeemer

f. Prince of Peace

7. Has your perspective of God changed as you have examined who He is in Scripture?

8. What does this mean in your present circumstances?

Join me again as we pray for our journey:

Heavenly Father, we come before You, our Sovereign and Holy God. Please reveal Yourself to us through Your Word. Make Yourself known in a specific way so that we know that it is You who is at work in our midst. Thank You that You are the One who redeems us from the pit of darkness and despair, You are the One who delivers us from our sorrow and pain, You are the One who brings peace in the midst of a storm, and You are the One who will fill all the empty and hurting places in our hearts. Show us in very real ways how wide and high and deep and long is Your love. We ask this in Jesus' name. Amen.

CHAPTER THREE
GOD'S STORY UNFOLDS

1. Which statement below best describes how you feel about the Bible?

    a. I have never read it.

    b. I have read it some but do not understand it.

    c. It is an interesting history/storybook.

    d. I use it as a guide for living, but I also look to other sources for truth.

    e. It is my daily bread. It is the only Truth by which I live my life.

2. Read the following Scriptures and then explain in your own words what each says about the Bible.

    a. 2 Timothy 3:16–17

    b. 2 Samuel 22:31 and Proverbs 30:5

    c. Matthew 24:35

    d. Psalm 119:89–91

3. Read Hebrews 4:12.

    a. What does it mean when it says God's Word is "living"?

    b. What about "active"?

    c. The verse continues, "it penetrates even to dividing soul and spirit . . . judges the thoughts and attitudes of the heart." Have there been times in your life when you have read the Bible and experienced "penetration" and/or "judging"? If so, how did you respond?

    d. If you have not experienced the Bible in the way described above, why do you think this is the case? Are you now willing to allow God's Word to do this in your life?

4. Study the following Scriptures. Explain what each says about how God's Word is to relate to your everyday life. Are there any that speak to you personally?

   a. Romans 10:17
   b. 2 Timothy 3:16–17
   c. 1 Peter 2:2
   d. Proverbs 4:4–5
   e. Deuteronomy 6:5–9

5. After reading this chapter, has your opinion of the Bible changed? If so, how? If not, why not?

6. Are you willing to give God a chance to show you that His Word can affect and even transform your life?

   a. Read Isaiah 55:8–11. This passage promises that God's Word "will not return to [God] empty, but will accomplish what [He] desire[s] and achieve the purpose for which [He] sent it." What could this mean in your life?

   b. Read the following Scriptures and apply the promises to your circumstances.

      (1) Jeremiah 29:11. Will you trust that God has a plan for your future? If yes, write out steps you can take to walk confidently in that trust. If you cannot, explain why.

      (2) Romans 8:28. Will you believe that God can take the difficult circumstances in your life and work them for His and your good? Have you already seen evidence of the good? If not, what can you do to realize the promise of this verse?

      (3) Deuteronomy 8:2–4 and 2 Corinthians 4:17. Describe what Scripture says about how God uses difficult times in our lives. Have you experienced this or observed it in the life of another?

Let us pray together:

Heavenly Father, we come before You today as the Author of Life. We thank You that in You is all Truth. Thank You that Your Word is living and active, it is eternal, and it is unchanging. Father, take Your Word as I read and study it, and plant it in my heart. Help it to take root and to grow deep roots. Allow Your Word to penetrate all those places in my heart that I have been protecting, those places I don't want to let anyone in, even You. Father, make my heart tender to Your sweet words of life. Till the soil of my heart so it is ready to receive all You have to teach me. We ask all these things in Your Son's holy name. Amen.

CHAPTER FOUR
TREASURES IN THE DARKNESS

1. Isaiah 61:1 tells us that God sent His Son Jesus to "bind up the brokenhearted." The Hebrew word for "broken" in this verse means "to break into pieces, to crush, or to smash." God knows that tests and trials in our lives will bring brokenness and at times even crush our spirits. So in His great love, He provided hope for that brokenness.

   a. Has your heart ever been or is it now broken? What are the circumstances that brought you to that place?
   b. Does Isaiah 61:1 speak to you in your brokenness?
   c. The Hebrew word for "bind up" is *chabash*, which means to wrap firmly, like to wrap or to bandage a wound. What a great illustration that Jesus is our Healer. Share a time in your life or in the life of another in which Jesus put the broken pieces back together and held them close and tight while His healing process began.
   d. Read Psalm 34:18 and Psalm 147:3. What does God want you to know about His character in these verses?

2. Read 1 Peter 4:12 and James 1:2–4.

   a. What do these Scriptures tell you about the tests and trials you face in your life?
   b. Does this change your perspective?
   c. Apply the Truths found in these verses to your circumstances.

3. In this chapter, you learned about the refining process and the "Refiner's fire."

   a. Applying this Truth, look back on difficult circumstances you have experienced. Do you see how these circumstances may have been part of God's refining work in your life?

b. What specific impurities has the Refiner's fire removed from your life?

c. If you are currently in the Refiner's fire, what might God be saying to you through your trial?

4. Are you harboring anger against God for something that has happened in your past or something going on right now?

a. Prayerfully seek God and ask Him to help you discover the root of that anger.

b. Are you willing to release your anger and trust Him in the midst of His refining work? Write a prayer releasing any anger, bitterness, or resentment you may harbor in your heart.

5. In this chapter, you read about "treasures in the darkness." As you have walked in darkness in the past (or maybe you are walking through it right now), have you experienced treasures in your darkness? Have you seen the beauty of God in the midst of a difficult and painful trial?

6. Read Psalm 139:23–24. Ask God to test you and know your anxious thoughts and to show you if there is any offensive way in you.

a. What things did God bring to mind?

b. Are you willing to let God work to change those things in your life?

c. If yes, what practical steps can you take to change or remove these things from your life?

Pray the following prayer as you claim God's promises for your life:

Heavenly Father, it is so difficult to walk through darkness. You feel so far away. I feel so alone. Father, thank You for Your promise that You will never leave me or forsake me and that there is nothing in all creation that will ever separate me from the love I have in Your Son, Jesus. Thank You for Your promise that You will bring good out of anything that enters my life when I love You and trust You to use it for Your purposes. Lord, I cling to that promise now. I also claim Your promise that You have a plan and a purpose for my life, and it is to prosper and not to harm me, to give me a hope and a future. Walk ever so closely with me during this darkness, Lord, and show me the treasures. Thank You that You will bring beauty from ashes. I ask all these things in Jesus' name. Amen.

CHAPTER FIVE
ON THE MAT

1. List what brings you contentment.

2. List what steals your contentment and brings anxiety, stress, and worry.

3. What do you spend the most time worrying about?

   a. Which of these are under your control?

   b. Which of these are not under your control?

4. Read Philippians 4:6–7. This passage tells us not to worry but to pray about everything. Worrying is self-centered, counterproductive, and keeps our eyes on our circumstances. Prayer is God-centered and keeps our eyes on God, not our circumstances.

   a. When you honestly examine your heart, do you find that you worry more or pray more?

   b. Take one or more of the items listed in question 2 and commit to live out Philippians 4:6–7 by giving them over to God.

   c. Write out a simple prayer, giving these worries and anxieties to God. Below is an example:

   Father, I thank You that You are in control of all things and that You want to take my burdens and worries from me. I ask You to take away my worries about (finances, jealousy, raising children, self-esteem, etc.). Father, I commit these things to You, thanking You in advance that You will work out every detail, trusting that none of these things comes to me before they have passed through Your loving hands. Thank You for the peace You have promised me . . . *the peace that will quiet my thoughts and my heart and give me rest.*

5. Read Philippians 4:8. Paul writes that in order to keep out the anxious thoughts, we must replace them with better thoughts. We are to think on whatever is "true, and honorable, and right, and pure, and lovely, and admirable . . . excellent and worthy of praise" (NLT).

   a. Examine what occupies your thoughts most of the time.
      (1) Are they thoughts of thankfulness, goodness, and serving others, or are they thoughts of grumbling, complaining, and wondering why you did not get your way?
      (2) Do you dwell on the positive or the negative?
      (3) Do you count your blessings or your problems?
   b. If you are struggling in your marriage, list five praiseworthy qualities in your spouse.
   c. If your battle is with your children, list five excellent qualities in each child.
   d. If you are struggling at work, list five ways your job blesses your life.

6. Read 2 Corinthians 10:5. It tells us we need to "take captive every thought to make it obedient to Christ." We must be intentional about building a steadfast mind. Let's dig a bit deeper into what you did in question 4.

   a. Find a Scripture that speaks to your specific issue. You can do this by looking up the key word in the concordance in the back of your Bible. Your word might be *anger, bitterness, fear,* or *anxiety.*
   b. Write the Scripture God leads you to on a note card or sticky note. Place it where you will see it throughout your day.

c. Memorize this Scripture and make it your own. Repeat it as written or make it a prayer in your own words. Add it to the prayer written above. Stick with this verse until your mind is as familiar with it as your own birth date. After a few weeks, write what God has done in your mind and in your heart through the power of His Word and your prayers.

Clear your heart and mind and pray this prayer:

Heavenly Father, thank You that You and You alone are my Authority. I pray for the mind of Christ. I surrender my thoughts and ask that through Your Word and the power of the Holy Spirit, You help me take captive every thought to the obedience of Christ. Father, I desire to obey You above all else. Consequently, in this moment I give my heart, my soul, my body, and especially my mind to You. Convict me every time I return to my old thoughts. Make my heart tender to receive and recall all the new thoughts You are planting within me. Bring Your Word to mind each time the temptation comes to return to what is familiar. Allow Your sweet Spirit to fill and saturate every part of me so I desire only to please You in all I say and do. Thank You for the victory You will give me in this today. In Jesus' name I pray. Amen.

CHAPTER SIX
LEARNING FORGIVENESS

1. Have you ever resisted forgiving someone who hurt or disappointed you? Do you currently harbor a lack of forgiveness in your heart against someone?

2. For the person(s) listed in question 1, why is forgiveness difficult (e.g., you feel you always give in, this person has not taken responsibility for his/her actions, this person has not asked for forgiveness, this person will get off easily, this person repeatedly hurts you and/or others)?

3. Scripture teaches that forgiveness is not optional. Jesus died on the cross to save you from your sin. You did nothing to deserve His forgiveness. He gave it freely with no conditions attached.

   a. Read Luke 23:34. Jesus models His standard of forgiveness. You forgive not because the other person deserves or earns your forgiveness. You forgive because you have been forgiven. Prayerfully consider extending forgiveness to the person you find hard to forgive. Ask God to soften your heart and then pray the following prayer:

   Heavenly Father, Your grace amazes me. Thank You for dying on the cross for me when I was still a sinner. Thank You for suffering pain, humiliation, and rejection for me. Thank You that Your sacrifice was sufficient to forgive all my sin. I know my unforgiving attitude toward (name) has grieved Your heart. Forgive me for not extending grace and forgiveness the way You extended it to me. You know how he or she has hurt me, Father. I ask in the name of Your Son, Jesus, for the strength to forgive (name). I leave all my pain and hurt at the foot of the cross, and I ask You to begin your healing work in my heart and mind. Take away my selfish thoughts and fill me with thoughts that are pure, righteous, and praiseworthy. Amen.

    b. After you have prayed this prayer and meditated for some time on what Jesus has done for you, contact this person and ask for his or her forgiveness. Share what God has taught you through this exercise.

4. God's Word warns that harboring anger and bitterness in your heart causes deep trouble in your life. Often your unwillingness to forgive hurts you more than it hurts the person who hurt you. If you have places in your heart in which you have harbored a lack of forgiveness in the past or are currently harboring it, do you see the trouble Scripture warns about (affects other relationships, physical illness, unanswered prayer, thoughts of revenge, unforgiving heart pours over into other areas)? Have you experienced any of these effects?

5. To overcome these thoughts and attitudes, Colossians 3:12, 14 tells us to clothe ourselves with new ones: *compassion, kindness, humility, gentleness, patience, and love.*

    a. Choose one of the attitudes listed above and commit to grow in that area for the next week in your relationships, especially any relationships where you harbor anger, bitterness, or a lack of forgiveness. I encourage you to model what we have done before. Take the above verse from Colossians or another verse, write it down, memorize it, and make it a prayer.

    b. After one week, write down how your change of attitude affected you, the other person or persons, and your relationship(s) with them.

CHAPTER SEVEN
SURRENDERING YOUR STRONGHOLDS

1. In this chapter, you learned about strongholds. Mine was fear. There are many others (worry, lack of forgiveness, bitterness, addiction, prejudice).

   a. As you read this chapter, did the Lord reveal any strongholds in your life?

   b. If He did, does your stronghold control your day-to-day living? If so, how?

   c. What, if anything, have you done to try to overcome your stronghold?

   d. Has it worked?

2. Read Ephesians 6:10–17. Describe the pieces of armor listed in these verses. How do you think God intends for you to use the pieces of armor to protect yourself?

3. Read 2 Corinthians 10:3–5, Hebrews 2:14–15, and Ephesians 6:10–17. Explain whom your battle is against and how God's Word promises to empower you to be victorious in this battle.

   a. Satan's goal is to keep you imprisoned in your stronghold so you cannot live out the incredible plan God has for your life. Do you believe that your struggle is actually against Satan, not against your stronghold or the one who caused your stronghold?

   b. Will you trust God at His Word and surrender your stronghold? Will you agree to surrender any anger, hatred and/or bitterness you may have against flesh and blood on this earth (a parent, an attacker, a husband, a sibling, a sickness, or a circumstance)? Acknowledge that your battle is against

Satan, and arm yourself for battle against him, claiming each piece of armor and the power of God's love.

4. Scripture reveals more about God's love in John 3:16 (NASB)— "God so loved the world, that He gave His only begotten Son, that whoever believes in Him shall not perish, but have eternal life." John 10:10 says that Jesus gave His life so that you would have life and have it abundantly.

   a. Do you believe that God loves you?
   b. If you do not believe this, what causes you to doubt God's love for you?
   c. To be victorious in this battle, you must surrender your doubt. Are you willing to do this? Will you believe God at His Word that He loves you with an unconditional and everlasting love?

5. Have you ever given your whole heart to Christ? Have you ever surrendered your life to the very One who created it? Once you believe God's amazing love for you and accept His Son, Jesus, as your Savior, Scripture says you are a new creation . . . not just reformed or rehabilitated, but a completely new creation. All that is old (your scars, your fears, your old habits, etc.) is gone, and He makes all things new (2 Cor. 5:17).

   a. If you have not yet given your heart to Christ, what is keeping you from surrendering to Him?
   b. Write out a prayer or a plan as to what steps you need to take to be able to surrender your heart to God.
   c. If you have given your heart to Christ, are there old things in your life that are keeping you from enjoying the abundant life that God promises through Christ? List those things.
      (1) Do you need to let go of the things you listed above? Write a prayer surrendering them to Christ.

(2) Do you need to relinquish control over your circumstances? Will you trust God with those circumstances?

Taking all that you have learned in this chapter, let's pray together for God to help you walk victoriously:

Heavenly Father, I praise You and thank You for the love You shower on me each and every day. I thank You that even when I am not living in a way that pleases and honors You, You continue to pursue me. Thank You that Your Word is Truth and that there is Power in Your Word. Thank You that I do not have to live in bondage to my stronghold. Instead, I can live in the Power of Your Holy Spirit, filled with Your Love, thinking and reasoning with the Mind of Your Son, Jesus Christ. This day I stand in Your Armor—the Helmet of Salvation, the Breastplate of Righteousness, the Belt of Truth, the Sword of the Spirit, the Shield of Faith, and the Shoes of the Gospel of Peace—in my battle against the Evil One and every time he knocks at the door of my heart, I know he will flee in the Power and Name of Jesus Christ my Lord and Savior. I ask that You fill me every day with Your Love, make Your Presence real, and give me the strength to stand strong as I grow in the wisdom and knowledge of Your Word. Thank You that I can now live free of my stronghold and know the abundant life You have promised me in Your Word. Amen.

CHAPTER EIGHT
QUIET TIME

1. Has there ever been a person in whom you have clearly seen Christ?

   a. What was it that drew you to that person?

   b. More specifically, list the characteristics that distinguish that person from other people you know.

2. Read the story of Mary and Martha in Luke 10:38–42.

   a. Describe the personality of each sister.

   b. Do you identify with one of the women more than the other?

3. Jesus says, "Martha, Martha.... You are worried and upset about many things, but only one thing is needed. Mary has chosen what is better, and it will not be taken away from her."

   a. Martha simply wanted Jesus to tell Mary to help in the kitchen. Instead of giving her what she wanted, Jesus gently rebuked Martha. If you had been Martha, how would Jesus' words have made you feel?

   b. As you read His words, how did they make you feel? What did they speak to your heart about your life's priorities?

4. Jesus told Mary that her dilemma and her behavior toward Mary were caused by the fact that she was "worried and upset about many things." What are signs in your life that you are in a state of anxiety or worry? How does it affect you physically? Spiritually?

   a. Read Proverbs 3:5–6 and Philippians 4:6–7. What do these passages tell you to do with your concerns? What is God's promised result?

b. Read Matthew 6:25–34. Respond to this passage by personalizing the verses for yourself. Do the same for Matthew 6:31–34. For example:

I tell you, _____, don't worry about your life, what your daily needs are, or about your weight or your appearance. Is not living your life in Me and for Me more important than worrying about your daily needs and your appearance? Look at the creatures I have created. They do not worry about their needs because I, your heavenly Father, provide for them. _____, you are far more valuable to Me than they are. You are made in My image, created for My purposes. _____, will all your worries add a single moment to your life?

5. What do you think Jesus meant when He said, "Only one thing is needed. Mary has chosen what is better"?

6. Jesus did not want Martha to change who she was; He simply wanted her to make a change in her priorities. Mary chose to sit at the feet of Jesus before she did anything else. We all face distractions or barriers to our quiet time with God. Put a check by the one(s) with which you struggle:

a. Busyness
b. Trials/hardships: feeling like you cannot count on God due to your circumstances
c. Pride: not feeling like you need quiet time
d. Tiredness/weariness: cannot get up early
e. Depression
f. Unworthiness: feeling that God has more important things to do

7. Examine your priorities. Where does time at the feet of Jesus come into your daily activities?

8. Respond to what you have learned in this chapter. Commit yourself to working toward having a heart that "chooses what is better," a heart that will seek first the kingdom of God.

   a. Find a time of day when you can be alone with God. Find a quiet place, sit down, and commit to spend time with God in that place.
   b. Decide what you will do with that time. Here are some ideas: Open your Bible and begin to read God's Word for yourself; spend time praying, not only for your needs but also for God to reveal Himself to you; or find a devotional book and read it, asking God to speak to you.
   c. As you begin these steps, write in a notebook your prayers and/or thoughts about what you are learning.

Let's pray together:

Lord, please draw me to Your Word daily. Your Word says that faith comes by hearing and hearing by the Word of God. Father, as I commit to spend time with You, help me to hear Your voice. I commit my thoughts to You and ask that You would fill me with Your Truth as I seek You each day. Help me to tune out anything that conflicts with the Truth You desire to speak to me. Give me ears to hear and let Your Word dwell in me richly. Give me discernment to understand all You have to say to me. I ask this in the name of Your Son, Jesus. Amen.

CHAPTER NINE
PRAYER

1. Did you pray as a child?

   a. If you answered yes, how did your family incorporate prayer?

   b. If you answered no, why did you not pray as a child?

2. Do you pray now? Is it different from when you were a child? Describe your current prayer life. If you do not pray as an adult, explain why.

3. Read the following verses. How do these verses align with your thoughts on prayer and how you pray currently?

   a. Colossians 4:2

   b. James 5:16

   c. Psalm 46:10

   d. Ephesians 6:11, 17–18

   e. John 15:7

4. In this chapter, you learned about "breath prayers."

   a. Write your own breath prayer. Pray it over the next week. Place your prayer in familiar places to remind you to pray (on your computer, on your phone, on your dashboard, on a mirror, over the kitchen sink).

   b. At the end of a few weeks, write down what, if anything, God did in your life through the continuous praying of your breath prayer.

5. You also learned about intercessory prayer. Focus on one of the following intercessory prayers and watch God work:

   a. Do you have people in your life who are hurting? Find one person in particular for whom you can commit to pray, and invite God to use you in that person's life during this time and see what God does.

   b. If you are a parent, pray specifically for one of your children. Ask God for wisdom to guide you on how to pray (behavior, salvation, humility, self-confidence). Tell your child you are praying for him or her, and then pray with him or her.

   c. If you are married, pray for your spouse or your marriage. Ask God where your relationship may need healing, forgiveness, or growth; and commit to pray for that. Ask God to make your heart tender to your role, if any, in helping Him respond to your prayer.

   d. At the end of one month, write down what God has done in your life and your spouse's life.

6. Our prayer life grows as we practice and use it more and more. God rewards this growth: "Well done, good and faithful servant! You have been faithful with a few things; I will put you in charge of many things" (Matthew 25:23). As you begin to pray, take baby steps.

   a. Journal when you see God answering prayer or intervening in the places you have committed to Him in prayer.

   b. Look for places where He gives you more opportunities to pray for others, and join Him in His work.

7. Is there a place in your life in which you feel hopeless or feel that things will never change?

   a. Will you surrender that place to God right now? Trust God with your heart and believe Him at His Word that He will work this situation for your good and for His glory.

b. Write a prayer that boldly asks for what you would like to see God do with that place in your life. Pray in the powerful name of Jesus, promising God that He will receive all glory and honor as His will is accomplished and your situation is transformed.

Pray that God will help you deepen your prayer life:

Heavenly Father, I praise You as the source of all Truth, as the Author and Perfecter of my faith. Thank You for creating me to be in relationship with You. Thank You that You desire for me to come before You in prayer. I commit to deepen my times of prayer with You. Please meet me every time I open my heart to receive all You have to offer me. Bring the fullness of Your Spirit into my prayer time with You. Let me sense the power of Your presence. Show me that You are active and listening. I claim Your promise that when I draw near to You, You will draw near to me. May I be different because of the time I spend with You. Change me as a woman, as a wife, as a mother, as a friend, and as Your servant. Make me a blessing to all those for whom I pray. May I draw others to You because of what You are going to do through me. In Jesus' name I pray. Amen.

CHAPTER TEN
ABIDING IN CHRIST

1. Praying God's will is simply incorporating His Word into your prayers. John 15:7 says, "If you remain in me and my Words remain in you, ask whatever you wish, and it will be given you." The key to answered prayer is knowing God's Word. Take some time to find these verses and note what each says about God's Word.

   a. Deuteronomy 8:3
   b. Deuteronomy 6:6–9
   c. Deuteronomy 11:18–19
   d. Psalm 119:9
   e. Psalm 119:105, 130
   f. 2 Samuel 22:31; Proverbs 30:5
   g. Isaiah 55:11
   h. Hebrews 4:12
   i. James 1:22
   j. 2 Peter 1:19–21
   k. Matthew 24:35
   l. Jeremiah 15:16
   m. Colossians 3:16

2. The great news is that God desires to use human beings with all their faults, doubts, and flaws to accomplish His mighty work on this earth. Read Exodus 3–4:14. In this story, God is calling Moses.

   a. How does Moses respond?
   b. How does God respond to Moses?
   c. In your own life, what keeps you from doing all God may be calling you to do? Be honest. Write out your doubts, imperfections, fears, and struggles.

3. Read Jeremiah 1. Here is a man doubting his ability to do what God is calling him to.

   a. How does Jeremiah respond to God?
   b. What does God promise Jeremiah?

4. In these stories and many others, it is clear that God equips and enables the men and women He calls to serve. Many of the people He called doubted their abilities. The distinguishing characteristic is that they trusted God despite their fears, doubts, and concerns. In the end, they obeyed. Today, God seeks to use you to affect the sphere of influence within which He has placed you. Do you feel God calling you to something in your life and yet you are not responding in obedience?

   a. Is God calling you to spend time abiding in Him?
   b. Is God calling you to commit to worship with your family in church every Sunday?
   c. Is He calling you to change your lifestyle (eating too much, drinking too much, speaking foul language, spending too much money, worrying about what others think, yelling too much, etc.)?
   d. Is He calling you to join a Bible study or to start one in your church or neighborhood?
   e. Is He calling you to the mission field to spread His gospel?

5. Sit at God's feet and ask Him what you can do to be in complete obedience to His calling for you right now.

   a. List what is keeping you from obedience.
   b. Write a prayer committing your obedience to God.
      (1) Ask Him for an obedient heart.
      (2) Ask for strength, wisdom, and understanding to know where He is calling you.
      (3) Ask Him to remove any obstacles that are getting in the way of your obedience.

c. Pray this prayer often and note when you see Him changing your heart, removing obstacles, opening doors, and finally blessing your obedience.

CHAPTER ELEVEN
A NEW SONG

1. My prayer is that wherever you are on your faith walk, you have met God in a new way. As you have journeyed through this book, what is the most significant way God has spoken to your heart?

2. It is through prayer that we come to know Christ in fresh ways. Through the power of prayer, we are filled to the measure of the fullness of God. Spend time reviewing the prayers you have prayed and the commitments you have made throughout the time of this study. How have you seen God work? What have you learned about God? About yourself?

3. As we say our good-byes, please continue to spend time in God's Word. I invite you not only to study God's Word but also to experience it. Allow it to invade your heart, to soak into the marrow of your bones, to mold and change you from the inside out. Do not stop what God has begun in your heart. Open a book of the Bible today and begin your journey. And as you read over the next weeks and months, journal what God is doing in your heart and life. Watch for Him to speak Truth into your difficult circumstances, heal your brokenness, give clarity to your confusion, and provide hope in the midst of your desperation.

4. As you commit time to God, believe with all your heart that God will bless your obedience. That is His promise. If you are not sure where to begin, start by setting aside a quiet time with God each day that includes time in His Word and in prayer. Find a community of believers to encourage you and to hold you accountable. Finally, pray for eyes to see ways you can join God in His work around you.

HUSH

ISBN-13: 978-0-8024-4864-4

Hush exposes the harsh realities of childhood abuse, explains the pain it causes, examines the false beliefs it creates, and empowers survivors to begin a personal journey toward healing by breaking the silence.

MOODY
Publishers™

From the Word to Life

1-800-678-8812 · MOODYPUBLISHERS.COM

BREATHE

ISBN-13: 978-0-8024-4865-1

At least one out of every three women experience some form of sexual abuse or assault, and this violation will impact her relationship with parents, friends, spouses, children, and God. *Breathe* is also a helpful tool for those in a relationship with an abuse survivor by providing guidance, confidence, and encouragement as they seek to provide help and support.

MOODY
Publishers™

*From the Word **to Life***

1-800-678-8812 · MOODYPUBLISHERS.COM